The Informed Gardener Blooms Again

T0339101

The
INFORMED
GARDENER

Blooms Again

LINDA CHALKER-SCOTT

University of Washington Press ❧ *Seattle*

Copyright © 2010
by Linda Chalker-Scott
Printed in the United States of America
Design by Ashley Saleeba
25 24 23 22 21   5 4 3 2

UNIVERSITY OF WASHINGTON PRESS
uwapress.uw.edu

The paper used in this publication is
acid-free and meets the minimum requirements
of American National Standard for Information
Sciences—Permanence of Paper for Printed
Library Materials, ANSI Z39.48–1984.

LIBRARY OF CONGRESS
CATALOGING-IN-PUBLICATION DATA

Chalker-Scott, Linda.
The informed gardener blooms again /
Linda Chalker-Scott. — 1st ed.
    p. cm.
Includes bibliographical references and index.
ISBN 978-0-295-99001-9 (pbk. : alk. paper)
1. Landscape gardening. I. Title.
SB472.c343 2010
635.9—dc22

2009042205

Cover front: Sarah Dixon, *lluminated
Manuscript I* (detail), © 2008. Oil on paper,
18½ x 24½ in. Cover back: Sarah Dixon,
lluminated Manuscript II (detail), © 2008. Oil
on paper, 18½ x 24½ in. Interior illustrations:
Sarah Dixon, oil on paper, © 2008. Reproduced
by permission of the artist.

As much as I love to write, I could not have finished this book as quickly as I did without my family. My son Jack, my daughter Charlotte, and my husband Jim are my ultimate support system. This book is dedicated to them.

CONTENTS

❧

PREFACE

As a researcher and educator in urban horticulture, I enjoy sharing the science in this emerging field with diverse audiences who are passionate about plants. *The Informed Gardener Blooms Again* is a continuation of the evidence-based, practical gardening information first presented in *The Informed Gardener*. While the books differ in content, they are both based on current, relevant plant and soil sciences as applied to home gardens and urban landscapes.

Readers of *The Informed Gardener* already know that I began my plant science career as a theoretical, laboratory-based plant physiologist and slowly evolved into a practical, landscape-oriented urban horticulturist. This was not a gentle journey. I was terrified teaching my first section of Landscape Plant Management (after years of teaching General Botany and Plant Physiology)—would the students realize how little I knew about applied plant science?

But I began to pay close attention to landscapes in every context—from formal gardens to ecological restoration sites to traffic circles—and analyzing them for successes and failures. The failures were especially intriguing, given the Pacific Northwest's ideal climate for growing plants. Here I was able to make use of my plant stress physiology background to diagnose what was going wrong with so many landscape plants.

As my knowledge base and confidence grew, I began to challenge many of the traditional practices and products associated with selecting, transplanting, and caring for trees and shrubs. In researching the scientific literature, one thing became clear: many of these practices and products were based on those used for growing crops that are planted and harvested on a cyclical basis. The mainstays of many landscapes—trees, shrubs, herbaceous perennials, vines, groundcovers, and bulbs—can live for decades or centuries. In this regard, landscapes need to be seen and treated in a more sustainable fashion.

Sustainability has become one of those buzzwords that can set your teeth on edge. What does it really mean? In the context of this book, it means several things:

1 Sustainability means discovering and supporting the natural processes that keep your gardens and landscapes healthy and functional. This approach allows you to work with your plants and soil rather than trying to control them. As a result, you'll find that you don't need those special concoctions and contraptions that are so heavily marketed to home gardeners.

2 Sustainability means choosing plants and products wisely to conserve natural resources. If you have a small urban yard, for heaven's sake don't choose trees that are genetically

programmed to reach towering heights! Likewise, be cautious about purchasing nonnative plants, beneficial insects, or soil organisms. Inadvertently releasing what may be a nuisance or invasive species will create problems far beyond your property.

3 Sustainability means creating gardens and landscapes that don't require continual input of packaged fertilizers and pesticides. Not only does this protect your wallet but it protects your soil, your plants, and adjacent watersheds from contamination by excessive nutrients and toxic chemicals.

When considered together, these three tactics represent an environmentally and economically sustainable approach to caring for gardens and landscapes. My passion has been to transform the ecological, botanical, and other relevant sciences into readily understandable and applicable practices for gardening and landscaping enthusiasts.

Gardening has expanded far beyond growing flowers and vegetables in one's backyard. Now it includes conserving native plants, protecting and nurturing landmark trees, planting parking strips and traffic circles, and restoring degraded landscapes. Many times this means working with school children, neighbors, volunteer groups, and government organizations to collectively reclaim "the commons" that have been despoiled by thoughtless or selfish actions.

The Informed Gardener was my initial effort in making the science of gardening and landscaping accessible to nonacademic types. Happily, that book proved popular and went into a second printing only eight months after it was first released. Though most people seem to appreciate what it has to offer, one reviewer criticized it for only presenting scientifically validated information. This reviewer felt that a better balance could be achieved by including anecdotes and unsubstantiated literature.

But I do not give anecdotes equal footing with scientifically validated information. If I did, my coverage of a particular topic would become a hopeless mishmash of conflicting stories, leaving the reader to wonder what rational conclusion could possibly be drawn.

That being said, informal observations and anecdotes often provide solid jumping-off points for further, more rigorous, investigation. Research can confirm or dispel cause-and-effect relationships, refining our understanding of how things work. I recommend only those practices and products supported by reputable research, and these recommendations will evolve as the body of science behind them grows. So, although this book is composed of columns I've written over the past ten years, the columns have been updated if new information has emerged in the interim.

You may notice the lack of references in some of the chapters. Practically speaking, plant researchers investigate questions that are fundable through USDA grants, which focus primarily on the production of food and fiber species. Thus, research on ornamental plants has lagged behind that of agricultural crop and forest species. Sometimes crop and forest research has application to gardens and ornamental landscapes, and sometimes it does not. I've tried to make this distinction clear throughout the book.

I hope that you enjoy this book. I also hope that if you have questions, comments, or criticisms, you'll contact me. Being an informed gardener is a dynamic process through which all of us can learn.

The Informed Gardener Blooms Again

EVIDENCE-BASED
GARDENING

THE MYTH OF
FOLKLORE GARDENING

The Myth

*"Gardening practices used long ago
are even more relevant today."*

It's said that history repeats itself, and the same holds true for horticultural practices. Old knowledge is rediscovered and presented in a context in which it is perceived as being more natural and environmentally friendly than cold, clinical, modern science. Certainly, many of the chemical-heavy pest management practices so popular in the middle of the last century have been prudently replaced with lower-tech, holistic approaches. Understanding how systems work is crucial when one is making landscape management decisions; the specter of persistent pesticides in our soil and water has led us out of the "spray and pray" mentality. The organic approach has spawned products and practices that are often environmentally sustainable, economically feasible, and socially acceptable. Are our "new" best management practices to be found in the past?

The Reality

As in most paradigm shifts, there's a danger in discarding current practices and replacing them with not only the good but also the bad and the ridiculous. A successful, holistic approach to landscape management requires solid underpinnings of whole-plant physiology—a field that barely existed 100 years ago and continues to evolve. If we don't understand how a plant responds to environmental changes—which includes management practices—then we can't predict what will happen to that plant or to the landscape in the future.

It is in this context that we need to critically assess old horticultural "wisdom." Two of the questions we should ask are "Does the rationale behind the practice make sense given our current scientific understanding?" and "Does the practice actually have a significant effect?" Here are some simplistic approaches I found in a thirty-year-old, but still popular, book by a well-known garden writer:

- "[To feed trees,] poke holes . . . about ten inches deep . . . fill with lawn food." Most tree roots are within the top eighteen inches of soil; in compacted soils, they are even shallower. The deepest roots are used for storage and stabilization, while the fine roots (also called feeder roots) close to the soil surface are used for water and nutrient uptake. And why use lawn food, which is often high in phosphates (a nutrient not usually deficient in nonagricultural soils?)

᠅ "Empty coffee cans aid deep-down irrigation. Cut out both ends, place in holes dug every few feet, fill with gravel and water regularly." Ditto. The fine roots are near the soil surface. Irrigating in this way wastes a significant amount of water and neglects many of the fine roots.

᠅ "[Tree wounds] should be sterilized with a solution of two tablespoons of ammonia per quart of water and then covered with pruning paint." Treating living tissues with a bleach solution and then covering the area with an impermeable barrier inhibits the natural formation of antimicrobial compounds and wound wood.

᠅ "Plastic sheets placed between rows of flowers and covered with colorful gravel keep weeds down all summer and provide attractive bed covering." I find plastic sheets to be anything but attractive, but leaving aesthetics aside, the use of plastic sheet mulch decreases water and gas transfer between the soil and the atmosphere. This inhibits desirable plant roots from colonizing the area under the mulch. Weeds, however, will happily grow on top of plastic mulches once soil and weed seeds have blown in.

᠅ "Don't spare the rod! Striking a tree trunk with a stick or a rolled newspaper stimulates sap flow in early spring." Personally, I find violent approaches to gardening repellent. Moreover, while mechanical stress does elicit a number of plant responses, there's no evidence that this particular treatment has any such effect. This last piece of "wisdom" propelled me to do some research. I did find one reference to this "curious habit," which was "to whip trees to induce them to fruit better, this being done ritually on Good Friday."

It is astonishing that the more dubious elements of "folklore gardening" have not only persisted in practice but have grown in popularity. We should be open to the wisdom of the past, but not at the expense of critical thinking. Beating trees, for example, is hardly a practice grounded in scientific thinking, and being open to new or old ideas doesn't mean buying into unsubstantiated beliefs. There are few who would argue that the medical knowledge from past centuries is more advanced than modern medicine; we are continually honing the practices necessary for optimal human health. Likewise, we need to continually evaluate the effectiveness of horticultural practices—old and new—for providing the best plant (and planetary!) health care.

The Bottom Line

∾ Understanding how a plant adapts and responds to its environment is crucial in making good landscape management decisions.

∾ Practices grounded in science, not promoted through folklore and superstition, should be the basis of landscape management.

~ Critically assess "garden wisdom": Does it make sense? Does it actually work? Going "back to nature," in medicine or plant health care, shouldn't include quackery.

~ If your knowledge of plant science is shaky, consider taking basic classes offered through university Extension services or through professional associations.

References

Chalker-Scott, L. 2008. "The Myth of Landscape Fabric." In *The Informed Gardener*, 145–48. Seattle: University of Washington Press.

Chalker-Scott, L. 2008. "The Myth of Phosphate Fertilizer, Part 1." In *The Informed Gardener*, 111–15. Seattle: University of Washington Press.

Chalker-Scott, L. 2008. "The Myth of Phosphate Fertilizer, Part 2." In *The Informed Gardener*, 116–19. Seattle: University of Washington Press.

Chalker-Scott, L. 2008. "The Myth of Wound Dressings." In *The Informed Gardener*, 198–203. Seattle: University of Washington Press.

Original article posted in May 2005.

THE MYTH OF
COMPANION PLANTINGS

The Myth

"Certain species will thrive, lean on, nestle with,
and support each other in groupings."

Anthropomorphism—assigning human characteristics to other species—allows people to feel more connected to the rest of the living world. Who hasn't bestowed their pet with human characteristics? It is in this context that the notion of "companion plants" first evolved many centuries ago. Historically, plants were associated with the four elements (earth, air, fire, and water) and signs of the zodiac. One of the outcomes of this categorization was the agricultural practice of planting together those species that "love" each other (an anthropomorphism reflected in the titles of at least two popular books on companion plants). The term "companion plant" has since entered the vernacular of both science and pseudoscience, so that its meaning is unclear. Is the concept of companion planting a legitimate horticultural practice?

The Reality

The problem with the term "companion plants" is that it is broadly used to describe plant interactions in the realms of science, pseudoscience, and the occult. A Google search of the phrase turns up nearly 30,000 hits on every type of Web site imaginable—but only slightly more than 500 of these are .edu sites. On such sites and in the scientific literature there are credible and intriguing studies demonstrating the mutualistic relationships among companion plants and their associated, beneficial insects and microbes. On less credible sites and in some popular books are the pseudoscientific claims that companion plants can be determined by "sensitive crystallization" of their extracts (i.e., determining which plants "love" each other) or through study of a plant's "rhythm, its vibration, its music, and its note" (Dengel 2009). When the science gets lost in the supernatural, then it's time for academicians and professionals to consider using different terminology.

Fortunately, there are several alternate terms with precise definitions that can be used in lieu of companion planting. "Intercropping" and "polyculture" are commonly used to describe agricultural production methods using mutually beneficial species. Ecologists use "plant associations" to define natural relationships among plants in nonagricultural situations. This latter phrase is my own choice for discussing the science behind plant interactions.

Plants, being immobile, must either adapt to their environment or alter it to survive. The alterations are often physical or chemical in nature. The mere presence of a single plant will modify environmental variables, including temperature, soil moisture content, soil pH, solar radiation availability (quantity and quality of light), and nutrient availability. These changes can affect the ability of other plants to survive; those that have a narrow range of tolerance for environmental change will be less adapted to their new environment and may die out. Other species that can tolerate or even require the changes can become established in their stead. Thus, a landscape will pass through successional changes as the interactions among the living components continue to modify environmental factors. Changes that affect multiple species in positive ways can often develop into mutually beneficial associations among those species.

This is the big picture. It might help to look at a specific example to see how the concept of companion plants arose. In North America, Indians historically planted corn, beans, and squash together in an intercropping system called "Three Sisters." Beans are nitrogen-fixers and continually supply this macronutrient to the soil. Corn stalks provide structure for beans to climb, and squash vines create a living mulch with their broad leaves that shade the soil, reducing evaporation and inhibiting weed seed germination. These three species have similar environmental requirements and don't outcompete each other for water and nutrients, thus allowing all three species to survive in the same space.

Researchers have documented several benefits in planting and maintaining diverse plant associations. Much of the work in this area has studied the effect of plant associations on insects. Diverse plantings will attract and retain beneficial insects, including the predator and parasitoid species so important for IPM

(Integrated Pest Management) and PHC (Plant Health Care) strategies. Furthermore, the presence of several species in a given area disrupts the ability of many herbivorous insects to discover their appropriate host plants for feeding or egg laying, primarily through visual miscues. In theory, time wasted on nonhost plants reduces reproductive efficiency of specialist insects, as they consume metabolic resources on aborted host selection events. Interestingly, some studies have reported that traditional "companion plants," including aromatics such as *Mentha* spp., have little or no disruptive effect on insect behavior, and can even exacerbate pest problems.

Further research on plant relationships beneath the ground has revealed that many plants share root system connections, primarily through mycorrhizal relationships. Mycorrhizae can transfer nutrients such as nitrogen between plant species, facilitating the growth of the receiver plant. Often, these receiver plants are completely dependent on these associations during some stage of their life and cannot survive without the donor.

There are other plant interactions that benefit at least one of the partners. Some plants from arid climates accumulate salts and can be used as desalinating partners for salt-sensitive species, such as hydroponically grown vegetables. Others can accumulate and sequester heavy metals from soils, decreasing their toxic effects on other species; poplars, willows, and other wetland plants are particularly useful in this regard. Nitrogen-fixing species, from birch and alder trees to garden peas and beans, provide this nutrient to other plants and microbes in their immediate vicinity. Nurse plants—plants that provide shade, block wind, and moderate the microclimate—enhance survival of newly germinating seedlings. All of these beneficial plant associations have been documented through research and used in the management of agricultural, ornamental, and restoration landscapes.

There is no scientific basis, however, for any of the several lists that exist identifying "traditional companion plants." Like horoscopes, these lists may be fun to use, but they should not be perceived or promoted as scientifically valid any more than astrology. Furthermore, those of us who value the science behind our horticultural practices should avoid using the term "companion planting" for precisely the same reason.

The Bottom Line

∾ The phrase "companion plant" is too vague to be useful; "intercropping" and "plant associations" are more definable and credible.

∾ Documented benefits from plant associations include physical, chemical, and biological alterations that can improve the establishment and survival of desired plant species.

∾ Pseudoscientific, mythological, and occult applications of "companion plantings" are not scientific.

∾ Traditional "companion plant" charts have entertainment, not scientific, value.

References

Casey, C. 2005. "Companion plants for ornamental nursery stock conservation biological control programs." *Bulletin OILB/SROP* 28(1): 47–50.

Close, D. C., N. J. Davidson, K. C. Churchill, and P. Grosser. 2005. "Evaluation of establishment techniques on *Eucalyptus nitens* and *E. pauciflora* in the Midlands of Tasmania." *Ecological Management and Restoration* 6(2): 149–51.

Colla, G., Y. Rouphael, C. Fallovo, M. Cardarelli, and A. Graifenberg. 2006. "Use of *Salsola soda* as a companion plant to improve greenhouse pepper (*Capsicum annuum*) performance under saline conditions." *New Zealand Journal of Crop and Horticultural Science* 34(4): 283–90.

Dengel, L. "Dynamic plants for farming and healing." http://www.auroville.com/auroannam/anp/healing-plants.htm. Accessed April 22, 2009.

Finch, S., and R. H. Collier. 2000. "Host-plant selection by insects—A theory based on 'appropriate/inappropriate landings' by pest insects of cruciferous plants." *Entomologia Experimentalis et Applicata* 96(2): 91–102.

Germeier, C. U. 2006. "Competitive and soil fertility effects of forbs and legumes as companion plants or living mulch in wide spaced organically grown cereals." *Biological Agriculture and Horticulture* 23(4): 325–50.

Held, D. W., P. Gonsiska, and D. A. Potter. 2003. "Evaluating companion planting and non-host masking odors for protecting roses from the Japanese beetle (Coleoptera: Scarabaeidae)." *Journal of Economic Entomology* 96(1): 81–87.

Liphadzi, K. B., and C. F. Reinhardt. 2006. "Using companion plants to assist *Pinus patula* establishment on former agricultural lands." *South African Journal of Botany* 72(3): 403–8.

McGee, P. A. 1990. "Survival and growth of seedlings of coachwood (*Ceratopetalum apetalum*): Effects of shade, mycorrhizas and a companion plant." *Australian Journal of Botany* 38(6): 583–92.

Moreau, T. L., P. R. Warman, and J. Hoyle. 2006. "An evaluation of companion planting and botanical extracts as alternative pest controls for the Colorado potato beetle." *Biological Agriculture and Horticulture* 23(4): 351–70.

Wilkinson, K. M. 2007. "Propagation protocol for 'iliahi (*Santalum freycinetianum*)." *Native Plants Journal* 8(3): 248–51.

Original article posted in July 2005.

THE MYTH OF
BIODYNAMIC AGRICULTURE

The Myth

*"Biodynamics is a scientifically sound approach
to sustainable management of plant systems."*

Biological dynamic agriculture, a.k.a. biodynamics, is a system of agricultural management based on a series of lectures given by Dr. Rudolf Steiner in 1924. Over his lifetime, Steiner became concerned with the degradation of food produced through farming practices that increasingly relied on additions of inorganic fertilizers and pesticides. Reputed to be the first alternative approach to agriculture, biodynamics has evolved to include many organic farming practices that have demonstrable benefits on land use and crop production; in fact, "biodynamic" is often used synonymously with "organic" in both scientific and popular literature.

Biodynamic agriculture has more recognition in Europe, but North American proponents of this system are increasing. Is the biodynamic approach one that should be encouraged?

The Reality

There are many nonscientific Web sites and writings about biodynamics, Rudolf Steiner, and the school of thought that he developed—anthroposophy. (An excellent scholarly overview by H. Kirchmann is referenced at the end of this chapter.) There are fewer refereed articles on biodynamics, and a review by Dr. John Reganold found many of these to be of questionable scientific quality.

Rudolf Steiner (1861–1925) was a true intellectual, with interests in many academic areas; his forte, however, was philosophy. The intention of his series of agricultural lectures was to instruct farmers how "to influence organic life on earth through cosmic and terrestrial forces" (Kirchmann 1994). This distinction is important, because biodynamic agriculture, as initially conceived, consisted primarily of concocting and utilizing eight biodynamic "preparations" that would "stimulate vitalizing and harmonizing processes in the soil" (Kirchmann 1994).

The directions for preparing the eight biodynamic compounds are complicated and can be found on a number of Web sites and in popular literature. Briefly, two of the compounds are prepared by packing cow manure (preparation 500) or silica (preparation 501) into cow horns and burying the horns for a number of months; the contents are then swirled in warm water and applied to the field. The cow horns are used as antennae for receiving and focusing cosmic forces, which are thought to be transferred to the materials inside. The other six compounds (preparations 502–507) are extracts of various plants either packed into the skulls or organs of animals (i.e., deer bladders and cow peritonea and intestines) or into peat or manure, where they are aged before being diluted and applied to compost. The chemical elements contained in these preparations are said to be carriers of "terrestrial and cosmic forces" and to impart these forces to crops and thus to the humans that consume them.

These processes were not developed through scientific methodology but rather through Steiner's own self-described meditation and clairvoyance. In fact, Steiner declared that these spiritualistically determined methods did not need to be confirmed through traditional scientific testing but were "true and correct" unto themselves (Kirchmann 1994). The rejection of scientific objectivity in favor of a subjective, mystical approach means that many of Steiner's biodynamic recommendations cannot be tested and validated by traditional methods. In practical terms, this means that any effect attributed to biodynamic preparations is a matter of belief, not of fact.

Muddying the discussion of biodynamics even further is the incorporation of organic practices into Steiner's original ideas. Many of these practices—no-till soil preparation, the use of compost, and polyculture—are effective alternative methods of agriculture. These practices have often demonstrated positive effects on soil structure, soil flora and fauna, and disease suppression, as they add organic matter and decrease compaction. Combining beneficial organic practices with the mysticism of biodynamics lends the latter a patina of scientific credibility that is not deserved. Many of the research articles that compare biodynamic with conventional agriculture do not separate the biodynamic preparations from the organic practices—and, of course, obtain positive results for the reasons mentioned earlier. Most recently, when researchers have directly compared parameters related to biodynamic and organic methods, biodynamic methods are no different from, or inferior to, organic methods. (On the lack of difference between biodynamic and organic methods, see Jayasree and George 2006; Radhakrishnan et al. 2006; Reeve et al. 2005; and Scarpa et al. 2008. On biodynamic methods as inferior, see Lam and Fernandez 2007; Stepien and Adamiak 2007; and Valdez and Fernandez 2008.) Other nonscientific practices have become part of the post-Steiner biodynamic movement. These include the use of cosmic rhythms to schedule various farm activities and nutritional quality "visualization." This latter practice uses legitimate chemical analyses such as chromatography as ways to study the "etheric" life forces in plants through "sensitive crystallization" and "capillary dynamolysis"—techniques that are again not scientifically testable.

Given the thinness of the scientific literature and the lack of clear data supporting biodynamic preparations, it would be wise to discontinue the use of the term "biodynamic" when referring to organic agriculture. I am guessing that many academics, both theoretical and applied, have no idea where the roots of biodynamic agriculture lie: the fact that "biodynamic" is used interchangeably with "organic" in the literature seems to support this conclusion. For me and many other agricultural scientists, usage of the term is a red flag that automatically calls into question the validity of whatever else is being discussed.

The onus is on academia to keep pseudoscience out of otherwise legitimate scientific practices. As Robert Beyfuss (New York Cooperative Extension) and Marvin Pritts (Cornell University) state, "It is this type of bad science that has created a hostility between the scientific community and many proponents of biodynamic gardening." All too often, scientists avoid addressing the problems associated with pseudoscience. Those scientists who do challenge pseudoscience are frequently attacked and ridiculed, thus shifting the focus from the problem (pseudoscience) to the personal level. This is partly a cultural shift. Alan Alda is quoted as saying "We're in a culture that increasingly holds that science is just another belief." But, more importantly, when published research is not held to an acceptable standard of scientific rigor and when junk science is not challenged, pseudoscience creeps closer toward legitimacy in the public eye.

The Bottom Line

⁊ Biodynamic agriculture originally consisted of a mystical, and therefore unscientific, alternative approach to agriculture.

⁊ The recent addition of organic methodology to biodynamics has resulted in a confused mingling of objective practices with subjective beliefs.

⁊ When subjected to scientific study, biodynamic preparations show no improvement over organic methods, and in most cases are significantly inferior to organic methods.

⁊ Many organic practices have been scientifically tested and can result in improved soil and plant health parameters.

⁊ The academic world needs to address the explosion of pseudoscientific beliefs and help nonacademicians become more discerning learners.

References

Kirchmann, H. 1994. "Biological dynamic farming—An occult form of alternative agriculture?" *Journal of Agricultural and Environmental Ethics* 7:173–87.

Lam, D. T., and P. G. Fernandez. 2007. "Soybeans under organic, biodynamic and chemical production at the Mekong Delta, Vietnam." *Philippine Journal of Crop Science* 32(2): 49–62.

Radhakrishnan, B., Q. R. Kumar, M. N. K. Ganapathy, and J. B. Hudson. 2006. "Effect of conventional, organic and biodynamic farming systems in tea." *Journal of Plantation Crops* 34(3): 330–33.

Reeve, J. R., L. Carpenter-Boggs, J. P. Reganold, A. L. York, G. McGourty, and L. P. McCloskey. 2005. "Soil and winegrape quality in biodynamically and organically managed vineyards." *American Journal of Enology and Viticulture* 56:367–76.

Reganold, J. 1995. "Soil quality and profitability of biodynamic and conventional farming systems: A review." *American Journal of Alternative Agriculture* 10(1): 36–45.

Scarpa, R., M. Thiene, and F. Marangon. 2008. "Using flexible taste distributions to value collective reputation for environmentally friendly production methods." *Canadian Journal of Agricultural Economics* 56(2): 145–62.

Smith, D., and J. Barquin. 2007. "Biodynamics in the wine bottle." *The Skeptical Inquirer*. http://www.csicop.org/si/2007–06/smith.html. Accessed April 22, 2009.

Valdez, R. E., and P. G. Fernandez. 2008. "Productivity and seed quality of rice (*Oryza sativa* L.) cultivars grown under synthetic, organic fertilizer and biodynamic farming practices." *Philippine Journal of Crop Science* 33(1): 37–58.

Original article posted in September 2004.

WHAT'S WRONG WITH MY PLANT?
AN INITIAL GUIDE TO DIAGNOSIS

1   Determine if a problem really exists. Be sure that you know exactly what your plant is and what it normally looks like. Many plants naturally have yellow or variegated leaves, peeling bark, or other characteristics that can be mistaken for damage. Many people don't know that larches and bald cypress are deciduous conifers that shed their leaves every fall, and instead think their tree is dying.

2   Be sure that your plant's location matches its environmental requirements. Shade lovers planted in full sun or drought-sensitive species planted in dry soils will suffer chronic environmental stress. Moving plants can often solve the problem. I had some roses that a previous owner had planted on the north side of our house, whose blooms suffered from severe fungal infection all summer. When they were dug up and reinstalled on the sunny south side of the house, the problem completely disappeared.

3   Make a list of everything that's been done in the vicinity of the plant over the last several years. This should include information such as:

෨   When the plant was installed, including the season

෨   How the plant was installed (e.g., were all materials removed from the root? Is the plant at grade, or is its root crown buried? Was the soil amended?)

෨   Activities that required removing significant amounts of soil, such as installing a sidewalk or a pond

෨   Activities that significantly changed drainage patterns of the landscape, especially those that may have caused compaction of the soil

෨   Fertilizer and pesticide usage

- ❧ Animal and human activities that might affect the plant or the surrounding soil

4 Look for damage patterns:

- ❧ A uniform damage pattern (e.g., damage on all leaves of a certain age or on all plants in an area) usually indicates nonliving factors, such as temperature fluctuations or water availability.

- ❧ An irregular or random damage pattern can indicate living factors, such as pathogens, insects, or other animals. However, many nonliving environmental factors are not experienced uniformly by the plant, and therefore damage will not be uniform. (For example, newly expanding leaves on evergreen species can be severely damaged by temperature extremes, while surrounding mature leaves are unaffected.) Damage by living organisms can be further characterized:

  a Viruses usually create a mottled pattern on leaf tissues, where streaks of yellow and white appear randomly. This phenomenon also occurs in floral tissues and has been exploited by plant breeders to develop unusual cultivars of tulips.

  b Fungi usually create a bull's-eye pattern on leaf tissues, with a dark spot in the center surrounded by concentric rings of progressive damage.

  c Bacteria usually cause a speckled pattern on leaf tissues.

  d Missing tissues from leaves or other plant parts indicate damage from insects or other herbivores. You may also find frass (insect waste) or webbing (not to be confused with spider webs) on the leaves.

5   Look for spread of damage over time.

ᔓ   Damage caused by an acute environmental stress (such as an early
    or late frost or unusually hot temperatures) will not spread to other
    parts of the affected plant or to other plants.

ᔓ   Progressive spread of the damage on a plant or onto other plants
    suggests either a chronic environmental stress (such as lack of water)
    or damage caused by living organisms.

6   Use other resources to confirm your diagnosis. You may need to hire
    a certified arborist or other plant professional to double-check your
    detective work. Alternatively, you may need to send a soil sample to a
    lab, or send a plant sample to your county Extension office, to obtain
    further information.

UNDERSTANDING
HOW PLANTS WORK

THE MYTH OF
FOLIAR FEEDING

The Myth

*"Fertilizers sprayed on the leaves of trees and shrubs
are more effective than those applied to the soil."*

Recently, I received an e-mail from a professional colleague whose clients often ask about foliar feeding as a method of fertilizing plants. "All the water-soluble fertilizer companies advertise the practice all the time," he said. What, he wondered, was my opinion of the practice?

Foliar feeding involves spraying the foliage of target plants with water-based fertilizers. The logic for the practice is based on scientific research from the 1950s, which demonstrated that leaves can take up minerals through their stomates, and in some cases through their cuticles. This research is consistently cited in the argument that foliar feeding is eight, ten, or even twenty times more effective than traditional soil applications. There are many enthusiastic proponents of foliar fertilizer use on shrubs and trees. It's preferred over soil fertilizers (say proponents), as you will see "immediate results" in "prolonged bloom" and "increased crop yields and storage life." Furthermore, they claim, foliar sprays will "maximize plant health and quality," and are effective at "boosting growth during dry spells," "increasing cold and heat tolerance . . . and pest and disease resistance," and "helping the internal circulation of the plant." It can be applied throughout the year, as long as it's not too hot or too cold, whenever "a quick growth response is desired" or during "any time of stress." As one company states, "In our opinion, foliar feeding is by far the best approach to use to insure maximum growth, yields, and quality by overcoming limitations of the soil and its ability to transfer nutrients into the plant."

The Reality

Foliar feeding is yet another agricultural practice best suited to intensive crop production under specific soil limitations. Advertisers take great liberties with the facts, often resulting in contradictory messages (such as time of application) or mysterious phenomena (I am most intrigued with "helping the internal circulation of the plant"). Rather than individually refuting the numerous errors in these claims, I'll explain when foliar feeding might actually be beneficial.

The original 1950s research came from Michigan State University and was particularly useful in understanding how nutrients move within plant tissues. As explained by Dr. Harold Tukey in his testimony to the Joint Committee on Atomic Energy, use of radiolabelled nutrients allowed his team to discover "that a leaf is a very efficient organ of absorption. The amounts may at first seem relatively small, but to offset this handicap, the efficiency is high" (Tukey 1956). From this, advertisers claim that foliar feeding is eight, ten, or twenty times more effective than soil application. This is not accurate for several reasons.

Obviously, materials applied directly to a leaf are more likely to enter the leaf in large quantity than the same materials applied to the soil. Leaching, chemical reactions, microbial activity, and so on can decrease the amount of material that reaches the roots and is taken up into the plant. But materials applied to the leaf do not necessarily travel throughout the entire plant as effectively as they do through root uptake. Instead, they often remain in the same or adjoining tissues and do not travel beyond the leaf. This is especially true of those elements recognized as "immobile" within plant tissues. While all minerals are freely transported through the roots and xylem, immobile elements can no longer be transported once they are incorporated into plant cells.

Research over many decades has explored the mineral uptake and transport of many species of fruit trees, conifers (including pine and spruce species), and some hardwoods of ornamental or commercial value. Results have been mixed, with some species responding well to treatment and others remaining unaffected. Generally, the results suggest that foliar application of particular nutrients can be useful in crop production when soil conditions limit nutrient availability. For instance, alkaline soils do not readily release many metallic nutrients. Iron and manganese are especially difficult for plants to take up under alkaline conditions. Zinc, copper, magnesium, molybdenum, boron, and calcium are other micronutrients required in small quantities. These nutrients have been applied to foliage in an effort to relieve deficiencies and combat deficiency-related disorders in commercial fruit production. Fruit, being adjacent to leaves, can benefit from foliar sprays. But this localized application does not affect the trunk or roots—and therefore is not a solution for soil imbalances. Researchers consistently state that foliar treatments are a specialized, temporary solution to leaf and fruit deficiencies in tree fruit production but will not solve larger soil fertility problems.

Macronutrients, which include nitrogen, phosphorus, and potassium, are needed by plants in larger quantities. While many of these macronutrients are able to move throughout the plant, it is pointless to apply them to foliage, as leaves cannot take up enough of them to supply the entire plant's demands. Furthermore, foliar application of high concentrations of such nutrients often results in leaf burn as water evaporates and the fertilizer salts remain behind, and substituting more numerous, lower concentration applications would not be cost effective.

Species differ widely in their ability to take up nutrients through their leaves. Differences in cuticle (the waxy covering of leaves) thickness, stomatal resistance (a measurement of how easily water and gas move into and out of leaves), and other genetic factors will influence uptake, as will environmental conditions. Plants in a protected situation (such as a greenhouse) have thinner and more porous cuticles than plants in the field, and take up foliar sprays much more readily. Likewise, plants adapted to arid environments naturally have thicker, less penetrable cuticles than those from more moderate climates.

A better solution to the problem of nutrient availability is to choose plants that can adapt to the existing soil conditions. If you have alkaline or calcareous soils, for heaven's sake don't install acid-loving plants! Poor plant selection in terms of mineral nutrition will be an upkeep problem for the lifetime of the plant— which may be pretty short. In these cases, choose cultivars of species that are more resistant to alkaline soils—they are able to acidify the root environment so that micronutrients are remobilized from the soil and available for uptake.

The existing research does not justify foliar fertilization of landscape plants as a general method of mineral nutrition. It can be useful for diagnosing deficiencies; for instance, spraying leaves with iron chelate can help determine if interveinal chlorosis is due to iron deficiency. Foliar fertilization would obviously benefit those landowners with landscape fruit trees that perpetually have flower or fruit disorders associated with micronutrient deficiencies. Applying fertilizers to leaves (or the soil) without regard to the plant's actual mineral needs wastes time and money, can injure plant roots and soil organisms, and contributes to the increasing problem of environmental pollution.

The Bottom Line

~ Micronutrients are the only minerals that are effectively applied through foliar application.

~ Foliar spraying is best accomplished on overcast, cool days to reduce leaf burn.

~ Tree and shrub species differ dramatically in their ability to absorb foliar fertilizers.

~ Proper plant selection relative to soil type is crucial to appropriate mineral nutrition.

~ For landscape plants, foliar spraying can be done to test for nutrient deficiencies, but not to solve them.

❧ Foliar application will not alleviate mineral deficiencies in roots or subsequent crown growth.

❧ Foliar spraying is only a temporary solution to the larger problem of soil nutrient availability.

❧ Minerals (especially micronutrients) applied in amounts that exceed a plant's needs can injure or kill the plant and contribute to environmental pollution.

❧ Any benefit from foliar spraying of landscape trees and shrubs is minor considering the cost and labor required.

References

Baldi, E., M. Toselli, D. Scudellari, M. Tagliavini, and B. Marangoni. 2004. "Foliar feeding of stone fruit trees." *Informatore Agrario* 60(21): 43–46.

Bi, G., C. F. Scagel, L. H. Fuchigami, and R. P. Regan. 2007. "Rate of nitrogen application during the growing season alters the response of container-grown rhododendron and azalea to foliar application of urea in Autumn." *Journal of Horticultural Science and Biotechnology* 82(5): 753–63.

Bouvet, G. 2006. "Walnut blight-apical necrosis: Test of agronomic control." *Acta Horticulturae* 705:447–49.

del Quiqui, E. M., S. S. Martins, J. C. Pintro, P. J. P. de Andrade, and A. S. Muniz. 2004. "Growth and mineral composition of eucalyptus seedlings cultivated under conditions of different sources of fertilizers." *Acta Scientiarum Agronomy* 26(3): 293–99.

Murray, T. P., C. H. Darrah III, and J. G. Clapp Jr. 2007. "Vapor pressure osmometry for prediction of turf burn from foliar fertilization." *Communications in Soil Science and Plant Analysis* 38(3/4): 337–46.

Sanchez, E. E., S. A. Weinbaum, and R. S. Johnson. 2006. "Comparative movement of labelled nitrogen and zinc in 1-year-old peach [*Prunus persica* (L.) Batsch] trees following late-season foliar application." *Journal of Horticultural Science and Biotechnology* 81(5): 839–44.

Schreiner, R. P., and R. G. Linderman. 2005. "Mycorrhizal colonization in dryland vineyards of the Willamette Valley, Oregon." *Small Fruits Review* 4(3): 41–55.

Solar, A. 2003. "The effects of foliar nutrition containing various macro- and microelements on the growth and development of young grafted walnut (*Juglans regia* L.) plants." *International Journal of Horticultural Science* 9(2): 33–37.

Tukey, H. B., and S. H. Wittwer. 1956. "The entry of nutrients into plants through stem, leaf and fruit, as indicated by radioactive isotopes." In *Progress in Nuclear Energy Biological Sciences Series Six*, 106–14. New York: McGraw-Hill; London: Permagon Press.

Widmer, A., W. Stadler, and C. Krebs. 2006. "Effect of foliar applications of urea and boron on *Malus domestica* and *Pyrus communis*." *Acta Horticulturae* 721:227–33.

Original article posted in March 2005.

THE MYTH OF
NIGHT LIGHT

The Myth

"Unless you're a poinsettia, increased light can't hurt."

Two of the "quality of life" characteristics of an urban or suburban environment are healthy greenspaces and substantial night lighting. These two characteristics are most noticeable along streets and in parklands. One might expect that this additional light (especially high-intensity light) would aid nearby trees and shrubs by prolonging photosynthesis. This is undeniably effective in greenhouses—why not in landscapes? And even if it doesn't help, it certainly couldn't hurt?

The Reality

Anyone who grows poinsettias or Christmas cacti knows that controlled light exposure is crucial for flower-bud development. I heard a nightmarish story a few years ago about a student intern who inadvertently turned on the lights of a greenhouse dedicated to poinsettia production: the entire crop was ruined when flower initiation was delayed past the holiday season. Other than in the cases of these specialty flowering plants, however, the effects of artificial lighting on plants are rarely considered.

Plants that have evolved under a regime of seasonal changes are exquisitely adapted to these changes. While temperature and water levels can fluctuate dramatically throughout the year, changes in day length are constant and predictable. The summer solstice represents the longest day of the year—or, in the case of plants, the shortest night. As the summer continues, days shorten and nights lengthen. Temperate plants cue into this shift, and at a particular light-to-dark ratio will initiate biochemical changes to prepare for winter dormancy. An uninterrupted dark period is critical for this process, as well as for flower-bud initiation in certain plants. In general, the harsher the winter, the earlier these changes occur, thus allowing native trees in colder environments plenty of time to become cold hardy.

When urban trees, especially street trees, are exposed to extended light periods, those leaves and buds nearest the source perceive an endless summer—and keep on growing. While this phenomenon is difficult to see initially, in the autumn it is quite distinctive, as was first noted in the literature over seventy years ago. Leaves that continue to receive high levels of light retain their green color, while those leaves under natural conditions have already started to senesce and change color. When the first autumn frosts arrive, the green leaves die before the tree can scavenge their nutrients, as would normally happen during leaf senescence. High-intensity light sources, such as high-pressure sodium lamps, have the greatest impact on delaying leaf senescence and the subsequent dormancy of landscape trees. Lights of lower intensity, such as those used in landscapes, are probably not a significant problem. The moon does not have an interruptive effect.

What does this do to the health of the tree? While the long-term effects of altered light periods on street and other urban trees have not yet been studied, the loss of resources puts a small but repeated strain on the tree. This could be manifested by reduced growth, compared to similar trees in more natural environments, or by a die-off of the roots most closely associated with the affected branches. Trees growing under ideal conditions probably won't be affected, but those in more stressful locations (those with less water, poor soil, etc.) are more likely to become susceptible to other stresses or opportunistic diseases. And, of course, flowering can be disrupted in landscape plants just as it can in poinsettias.

The Bottom Line

❧ Artificially prolonged light periods can interrupt flowering cycles and delay winter dormancy.

❧ Marginally hardy plants should never be exposed to interrupted dark periods.

❧ Consider the location of high-intensity light sources (street lights, security lights, etc.) before installing shrubs and trees.

๛ The effects of high-intensity lights can be partially moder-
ated by installing deflectors on the lights.

References

Margolis, H. A., J. Begin, R. Beeson, and P. Bellefleur. 1988.
"The influence of metal halide and high-pressure sodium
lamps during photoperiod extension on the allocation of
carbon between lignin and cellulose in black spruce seedlings." *Canadian Journal of Forest Research* 18(7): 962–64.

Matzke, E. B. 1936. "The effect of street lights in delaying leaf-
fall in certain trees." *American Journal of Botany* 23:446–52.

Omi, S. K., and K. L. Eggleston. 1993. "Photoperiod extension
with two types of light sources: Effects on growth and development of conifer species." *Tree Planters' Notes* 44(3): 105–12.

Richardson-Calfee, L. E., J. W. Day, W. T. Witte, and D. C. Fare.
2001. "Effects of extended photoperiod and light quality on
growth of *Carpinus caroliniana, Fagus grandifolia* and *Gymno-
cladus dioicus* seedlings." *Journal of Environmental Horticulture*
19(4): 171–74.

Taylor, J. A. 1958. "London's plane. Some notes and observations." *Gardeners' Chronicle* 144:253.

Original article posted in February 2004.

THE MYTH OF
RED LEAVES

The Myth

*"If a plant develops red leaves, it means
that it is phosphorus deficient."*

The ability of some leaves to turn from green to red, or from red to green, has intrigued people for millennia. Every spring, one sees new leaves emerging from buds on deciduous shrubs and trees; many of these buds and young leaves are red. Leaf reddening continues in a variety of plant species throughout the year, ending with autumn's showstopping display. The appearance of red leaves in corn and other crops during the growing season, however, often indicates phosphorus deficiency. Nitrogen, phosphorus, and potassium—the N-P-K on fertilizer labels—are the most commonly deficient nutrients in crop production. Shouldn't we also fertilize our garden and landscape plants whose leaves inexplicably turn red?

The Reality

Leaf reddening is caused by the production and accumulation of anthocyanins, which are water-soluble pigments that may impart a red, blue, or purple coloration to vegetative tissues (and flowers as well). There are a number of reasons these pigments are produced in leaves, including:

- NORMAL JUVENILE REDDENING. Many plants, including *Photinia*, produce young red leaves. These leaves turn green upon reaching full size. This is a natural phenomenon.

- NORMAL RED LEAF MORPHOLOGY. Other plants, including some *Acer* species, produce red leaves that maintain their redness even in maturity. These are often desirable cultivars because of the distinctive coloration of the leaves.

- DROUGHT. Lack of sufficient water in plant leaves commonly induces anthocyanin production. While the exact mechanism is unclear, it is likely that these water-soluble pigments help conserve the remaining leaf water.

- SALT STRESS. Like drought, the presence of salt in soil, water, or the atmosphere will cause a dehydration of leaf tissues and a resultant formation of anthocyanins.

- NUTRIENT DEFICIENCY OR TOXICITY. Many essential nutrients and nonnecessary minerals can cause leaf reddening if they are deficient or in excess. Phosphate deficiency is one of the least likely deficiencies in nonagricultural landscapes.

  ✺ COLD TEMPERATURES. Cold temperatures can decrease water uptake, leading to low-water conditions in leaves. Furthermore, freezing inside the leaves will decrease the amount of water available in a liquid form and cause a freeze-induced dehydration.

  ✺ HYPOXIA. This condition, in which the oxygen level is lower than normal, is common in urban areas, where compacted and poorly drained soils contain too little oxygen for root systems to survive. Without living roots, water uptake decreases, and leaf-water deficit occurs.

  ✺ WOUNDING. Wounding by animals, people, or vehicles can induce a localized reddening response.

  ✺ PATHOGENS. Exposure to many bacteria and fungi will induce anthocyanin formation.

  ✺ HERBICIDES. Inadvertent exposure to herbicides can also cause leaves to synthesize anthocyanins.

From this brief outline, it should be apparent that many environmental factors can induce leaf reddening. It is highly unlikely, especially in ornamental landscapes, that reddening is caused by phosphate deficiency. As I've discussed in *The Informed Gardener*, the overuse of phosphate in nonagricultural landscapes is dangerous to soil, plant, and ecosystem health.

How do anthocyanins alleviate environmental stress in leaves? There is no one answer, but evidence points toward a trio of functions: reduction of water loss, solar protection, and antioxidant behavior.

The Bottom Line

๛ There is no single reason why leaves turn red.

๛ The young leaves in many species, especially cultivated ornamental plants, are naturally red.

๛ Many environmental factors can induce leaf reddening.

๛ In nonagricultural landscapes, phosphate deficiency is not likely to occur and therefore will generally not be a cause of leaf reddening.

๛ Before adding phosphate fertilizer, have a soil test performed to assess phosphorus availability.

References

Chalker-Scott, L. 2008. "The Myth of Phosphate Fertilizer, Part 1." In *The Informed Gardener*, 111–15. Seattle: University of Washington Press.

Chalker-Scott, L. 2008. "The Myth of Phosphate Fertilizer, Part 2." In *The Informed Gardener*, 116–19. Seattle: University of Washington Press.

Chalker-Scott, L. 2002. "Do anthocyanins function as osmo-regulators in leaf tissues?" *Advances in Botanical Research* 37: 103–27.

Chalker-Scott, L. 1999. "Environmental significance of anthocyanins in plant stress responses." *Photochemistry and Photobiology* 70:1–9.

Original article posted in April 2002.

THE MYTH OF
STOIC TREES

The Myth

"Unless it causes visible damage, touching
or brushing has little effect on plants."

For those of us whose vocation or avocation includes sustainable gardening and landscaping, one of our core tenets is basing our practices on scientifically objective criteria. *The Informed Gardener* has tried to bring science to gardeners and has also identified questionable practices and products with no basis in science. Therefore, informed gardeners will be skeptical when they hear that plants respond to touch. Of course, damaging forms of contact, whether by herbivores or construction equipment, will elicit a response from plants. But plants responding to gentle stroking is a little too "touchy-feely" for many of us. Is this science or pseudoscience?

The Reality

Plants, being immobile, respond quite differently to their environment than do animals that can escape hostile conditions. Plant responses to touch (often termed "mechanical perturbation" or "MP" in the scientific literature) can be exquisitely sensitive. The ability of some carnivorous plants to actively trap food is an example of touch response, as is the leaf movement of sensitive plants (such as *Mimosa* spp.) and the coiling of vine tendrils. These are relatively rapid responses, compared to another type of touch response, called "thigmomorphogenesis." This word was coined several decades ago by one of the first researchers in the field of mechanical perturbation (MP) or plant touch responses, and is used to describe the long-term changes in the appearance of a plant ("-morpho-") in response to repeated touching ("thigmo-").

Thigmomorphogenesis can be induced by many types of environmental MP, including wind, water spray, snow load, and rubbing from other plants. People, wild and domesticated animals, and even insects can also cause these changes. The responses are species-specific in terms of the amount of MP required and the resulting morphological changes seen. Initially studied in annual crop plants, such as peas, beans, corn, and sunflowers, MP was universally seen to decrease stem elongation and increase stem thickness. Other characteristics include shorter petiole length, smaller leaves, fewer flowers, and increased senescence (programmed tissue death). Similar responses have been demonstrated in woody species including pine (*Pinus*), spruce (*Picea*), fir (*Abies*), poplar (*Populus*), and elm (*Ulmus*).

Continual rubbing or brushing of woody trees and shrubs, even when gentle enough not to abrade tissue, will result in shorter heights and wider trunks. This is partially mediated through the release of ethylene gas, a naturally produced plant-growth regulator, which in turn increases the formation of lignin (one of the plant biochemicals that contributes to the "woodiness" of some plant tissues) in the disturbed tissues. The result of thigmomorphogenesis is a stocky, sturdy plant that is more resistant to breakage or blowdown than one that has been untouched, and the greater the disturbance, the more pronounced the response. The short, stunted appearance of alpine forest trees is an extreme example of wind-induced thigmomorphogenesis. Such trees are less likely to blow down or break from snowload than are thin, upright specimens.

Thigmomorphogenesis is especially important to understand where landscape trees are concerned. While trees in the middle of a forest do not experience buffeting from wind, urban trees are likely to be isolated and exposed. Allowing these isolated trees to sway in the wind will increase their trunk girth and taper while keeping crown growth in check. Wind stress also increases root growth and stability, especially in shallow or compacted soils, which are common in urban areas. The result is a more firmly anchored tree with a reduced crown-to-root ratio. In contrast, improperly staked trees cannot sway in the breeze and therefore do not develop the girth, taper, or root stability necessary for surviving future wind stress. As discussed in *The Informed Gardener*, such trees are more likely to experience crown breakage or uprooting once the staking is removed.

The Bottom Line

๛ Plants exposed to continual touching by various environmental factors undergo thigmomorphogenic changes.

๛ Easily seen thigmomorphogenic changes in landscape trees include increased trunk diameter and decreased height.

๛ Improper tree staking will inhibit normal, wind-induced thigmomorphogenesis and will make a tree more likely to topple or break once staking is removed.

References

Autio, J. V., and T. Koivunen. 1994. "Responses of aster, dusty miller, and petunia seedlings to daily exposure to mechanical stress." *Hortscience* 29(12): 1449–52.

Berthier, S., and A. Stokes. 2005. "Phototropic response induced by wind loading in Maritime pine seedlings (*Pinus pinaster* Ait.)." *Journal of Experimental Botany* 56(413): 851–56.

Braam, J. 2005. "In touch: Plant responses to mechanical stimuli." *New Phytologist* 165(2): 373–89.

Cahill, J. F., Jr., J. P. Castelli, and B. B. Casper. 2002. "Separate effects of human visitation and touch on plant growth and herbivory in an old-field community." *American Journal of Botany* 89(9): 1401–9.

De Boeck, H. J., M. Liberloo, B. Gielen, I. Nijs, and R. Ceulemans. 2008. "The observer effect in plant science." *New Phytologist* 177(3): 579–83.

Jaffe, M. J., A. C. Leopold, and R. C. Staples. 2002. "Thigmo responses in plants and fungi." *American Journal of Botany* 89(3): 375–82.

Mickovski, S. B., and A.R. Ennos. 2003. "Anchorage and asymmetry in the root system of *Pinus peuce*." *Silva Fennica* 37(2): 161–73.

Nicoll, B. C., and D. Ray. 1996. "Adaptive growth of tree root systems in response to wind action and site conditions." *Tree Physiology* 16(11/12): 891–98.

Pruyn, M. L., B. J. Ewers, and F. W. Telewski III. 2000. "Thigmomorphogenesis: Changes in the morphology and mechanical properties of two *Populus* hybrids in response to mechanical perturbation." *Tree Physiology* 20(8): 535–40.

van Emden, H. F., R. J. Macklin, and S. Staunton-Lambert. 1990. "Stroking plants to reduce aphid populations." *Entomologist* 109(3): 184–88.

Original article posted in August 2005.

THE MYTH OF
DESIGNER TREES

The Myth

*"Landscape trees need to be headed back
in the nursery to develop proper branching."*

An increasingly common practice in production nurseries is the heading back, or topping, of young trees destined for landscape use. Juvenile trees generally display excurrent growth patterns, exemplified by a strong central leader but few laterals. When young trees are topped, one of the new resulting branches near the top is subsequently trained to become the leader. Frequently, the tree may be headed a second time. The increase in branching and lateral growth causes the tree to acquire a more mature (decurrent) appearance (see fig. 1). This appearance is important to consumers, who want to see what a tree will look like at matu-

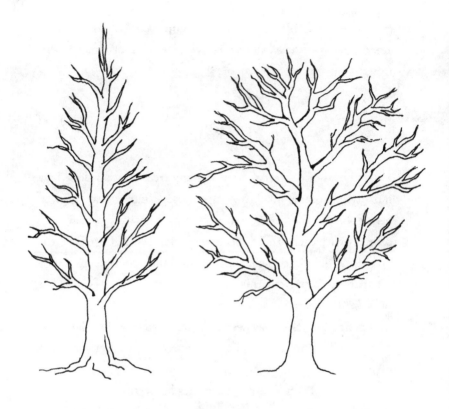

FIGURE 1.
Stylized drawings of mature excurrent (*left*) and decurrent (*right*)
trees. Note that the strong central leader of an excurrent tree is
replaced by a rounded crown in the decurrent tree as it ages.
Illustration by Doris Anderson.

rity. Heading back also facilitates controlled pollination and insect and disease management by keeping the branches of the tree within easy reach. This procedure originated well over 300 years ago as a way of improving the survival of bare-root seedlings. It is particularly useful for managing fruit trees and other species used for seed or fruit production. Leader heading at the production nursery is currently performed on many deciduous and coniferous species destined for landscape use rather than crop production. Is this practice of heading young trees appropriate for specimens used along streets and in other ornamental settings?

The Reality

The removal of the leader from a young tree, whether done by a nursery, a gardener or a browsing herbivore, induces new growth below the cut shoot. These new branches grow vigorously and compete with each other to become the new leader. Often there is no clear winner in this competition, and the tree develops multiple trunks. To prevent this undesirable effect (discussed in *The Informed Gardener*), a new leader must be selected and trained. Competing branches may need to be removed or trained laterally. These can be time-consuming and expensive tasks. As part of a management system for peach, apple, and other tree crops, it may be economically feasible, since it makes harvesting more efficient (though some recent research disputes the value, citing reduced harvests after topping). The only economic argument for heading young landscape trees in the nursery is to reduce shipping costs by decreasing height.

A second reason for this nursery practice is to create miniature "adult" trees designed to appeal to customers who are not aware of the natural differences between juvenile and adult morphologies. When faced with a choice between a whip-like sapling and one with branches, customers are likely to choose the latter, even when the crown is of poor quality and will need corrective pruning in the future.

A final reason for this type of pruning is to force young trees to conform to unrealistic tree specifications written by urban planners and landscape architects for use in public works projects. Installation specifications that require a large number of branches in young trees, especially in species that do not develop laterals as juveniles, encourage both the creation and the purchase of headed trees. On street trees in particular, low lateral branches will become nuisances to pedestrians and vehicles alike as they continue to grow. While gardeners may not be concerned with such specifications, the reality is that these specifications are used by growers to produce trees—and these trees will often be the only ones available at the local nursery.

As discussed in the first volume of *The Informed Gardener*, the practice of tree topping cannot be justified scientifically, especially with our increased understanding of tree physiology and hazard tree development. Multiple branches crowded along the trunk could theoretically become failure points as the tree grows, and there is no doubt that headed trees are aesthetically unappealing. Yet the practice of heading young trees continues to be recommended in print and on the Web. With such subjective statements as "some species do not branch effectively," enthusiasts claim that the continual heading of leaders and laterals allow one to "literally build a tree." However, there is no valid physiological reason to interfere with the normal growth patterns of young landscape trees by heading otherwise healthy leaders and laterals.

The Bottom Line

- Juvenile trees, especially decurrent species, usually exhibit excurrent growth until they approach maturity.

- Heading back any tree will result in vigorous, uncontrolled growth, which increases the maintenance costs associated with the tree, both at the nursery and in the landscape.

෧ If a particular species does not naturally have the desired branching as a juvenile, then another species should be selected.

෧ Tree standards and specifications should conform to tree biology; we should not expect trees to conform to artificial and unrealistic standards.

References

Chalker-Scott, L. 2008. "The Myth of Tree Topping." In *The Informed Gardener*, 43–48. Seattle: University of Washington Press.

Clair-Maczulajtys, D., I. le Disquet, and G. Bory. 1999. "Pruning stress: Changes in the tree physiology and their effects on the tree health." *Acta Horticulturae* 496:317–24.

Mock, T. 2002. "Nursery tree quality grades and standards." *Arbor Age* 22(10): 46.

Original article posted in February 2005.

THE MYTH OF
UNIFORM PLANT
PERFORMANCE

The Myth

*"Nursery tags will give an accurate
indication of final plant size."*

Tree selection can be a tricky practice, especially when site conditions constrain the size of the plantings. Parking strips, traffic
circles, pocket gardens, and other small landscapes require small-
scale plants. At the nursery, one can be overwhelmed by the variety of broadleaf trees and conifers, and even within a species
there may be several cultivars from which to choose. Without any
prior knowledge of these plants, consumers resort to trusting
nursery tags to indicate the mature height and spread. Armed
with this information, can one reliably select those trees and
shrubs whose scale is appropriate to the site?

The Reality

Many factors will determine the mature size of a tree or shrub. The most obvious influence on plant size is genetic makeup—you only have to look at cultivar names such as 'Midget' or 'Giant Candles' to understand this. Geographic location also plays a major role in determining a plant's height. For instance, trees tend to grow taller in areas where temperatures are more moderate; trees in coastal areas are generally larger than the same species in more continental regions. Within a geographic range, local climate will further influence final size; rainfall and temperature can vary widely within a region as a result of local topography. The microclimate of a site will influence tree size because of differences in environmental factors such as drainage, soil type, and aspect. Finally, competition for water, light, nutrients, and other essentials will affect not only a plant's growth rate but its final height as well.

To illustrate the interaction among these various factors, let's examine a common ornamental tree with an ancient lineage: *Ginkgo biloba*, the only extant species in the ginkgo family. *Ginkgo biloba* is an excellent choice for many urban landscapes, as it is relatively resistant to air pollution, insects, disease, and other environmental stresses. The first three taxonomic keys I looked at reported that *Ginkgo biloba* would reach (1) up to 100 feet, but usually less; (2) over 100 feet; and (3) 130 feet. Were I to visit a nursery to determine plant size, I might find a tag such as that from a Nebraska nursery giving a mature height of 40 to 70 feet. Looking on the Internet, I found U.S. state-champion ginkgoes from a number of locations:

- Tennessee state champion: 90 feet

- Alabama and Ohio state champions: 80 feet

- Texas state champion: 72 feet

- Arkansas state champion: 57 feet

- North Dakota state champion: 24 feet

And, in Japan, is a thousand-year-old specimen topping out at 164 feet!

Clearly, there is no one "mature size" for trees, especially when trees are grown outside their native habitat. From the state-champion data, it appears that colder climates (e.g., North Dakota) produce smaller ginkgoes, but other factors besides winter temperature influence mature size. (Why is the state champion of Tennessee so much larger than that of Arkansas?) The lack of consensus among tree identification guides, taxonomic literature, nursery tags, and real-life landscape specimens underscores the fallacy of assuming a uniform maximum height for any species, variety, or cultivar of tree or shrub. The geographic location of the information source (e.g., the production nursery or the tree-guide author) can greatly influence the reported attributes of the species in question.

So, how does one predict how tall a tree or shrub will become in one's landscape? The best way is to observe the plant of interest in your region: How tall does it get? How wide is its crown? After making such observations, you will have a predictive range of heights. Regional field guides might also have useful information. If there are not enough specimens in your area, or if they are not mature, explore the Web for information on plant performance in other geographic regions with similar climate conditions. Those of us in the moderate Pacific Northwest region know that we have a cool Mediterranean climate and can look to those countries for information on plant performance.

The Bottom Line

∾ There is great variability within print resources regarding mature tree height.

∾ Production nursery tags most likely contain species performance information relevant to that nursery's geographic location.

∾ Genetics, geography, climate, and plant competition will all influence the maximum height any specimen will obtain.

∾ To determine the most likely height range for a tree in your landscape, observe how that species performs elsewhere in your location.

∾ If no local landscape specimens exist for a particular plant, look to the Internet or regional field guides for plant performance information from similar climates elsewhere in the world.

References

Kang, H. 1991. "Components of juvenile-mature correlations in forest trees." *Theoretical and Applied Genetics* 81(2): 173–84.

Niklas, K. J. 2007. "Maximum plant height and the biophysical factors that limit it." *Tree Physiology* 27(3): 433–40.

Original article posted in November 2004.

THE MYTH OF
WILTING LEAVES

The Myth

"Leaf wilt is the best indicator of insufficient soil moisture."

With summer's longer days and increasing temperatures, plant growth and water demand steadily increase. One of the best visual indicators for adequate plant moisture is leaf turgor. (Turgor is the relative water content of tissue; wilted leaves have low turgor.) This makes sense, as leaves are the main destination points for water uptake, and up to 90 percent of transported water is lost through leaf stomates. When water availability lessens, the plant has a harder time extracting it from the soil, yet the leaves continue to require water for expansion, nutrient transport, and photosynthesis. The youngest and most tender leaves and shoots will be the first to show the effects of water stress by wilting, because their cell walls will not yet have lignified. Eventually, a permanent wilt point is reached—a clinical way of saying that the leaves or shoots are dead. Any gardener will want to avoid this problem, and therefore leaf wilt is often used as an indicator to increase water application. Unfortunately, this blanket approach to irrigation can often make the problem worse if lack of soil moisture is not the underlying cause of wilt.

The Reality

Leaf wilt can result from a number of stresses in the soil environment, many of which lead directly or indirectly to water deficits in the leaf. A common cause of leaf wilt in urban environments, especially sites with compacted, poorly drained soils, is root hypoxia. Soils without sufficient pore space are deficient in oxygen, which severely impacts root function. Roots, like any other living tissue, require oxygen for survival; since they are not photosynthetic, they rely on oxygen from the soil or from aboveground parts of the plant. Excess water will fill soil pores and eliminate gas exchange. Without enough oxygen, root function shuts down and water uptake ceases. Leaf transpiration continues, however, and eventually leaves will wilt as their water content decreases. Ironically, the leaves suffer from drought stress, even though soil moisture is more than adequate!

Other environmental factors besides soil compaction can cause root dysfunction and lead to leaf water stress, including:

ᴥ freezing temperatures in the root zone

ᴥ excessive heat in the root zone

- excess salts in fertilizers or the water source

- insect and rodent damage

- fungal and bacterial pathogens

- circling, girdling root systems

Some of these factors are most common in containerized plantings. Root hypoxia is probably the leading cause of death in houseplants and in plants in outdoor containers without adequate drainage. Obviously, one wants to ensure that water truly is the limiting factor before adding more to the root environment.

The Bottom Line

- Be sure to assess soil conditions before irrigating wilted plants.

- If the soil is wet, try to aerate throughout the root zone.

- If the soil is chronically wet, consider installing a French drain or other passive means of drainage. (At its simplest, a French drain consists of a narrow trench filled with stone. More complicated versions exist.)

- Alternatively, select trees and shrubs adapted to wet conditions.

References

Chang, T. T. 1995. "Decline of nine tree species with brown root rot caused by *Phellinus noxiu* in Taiwan." *Plant Disease* 79(9): 962–65.

Parke, J. L., R. G. Linderman, N. K. Osterbauer, and J. A. Griesbach. 2004. "Detection of *Phytophthora ramorum* blight in Oregon nurseries and completion of Koch's postulates on *Pieris, Rhododendron, Viburnum*, and *Camellia*." *Plant Disease* 88(1): 87.

Schooley, J., and J. T. A. Proctor. 2003. "Freeze damage to North American ginseng." *HortTechnology* 13(4): 697–701.

Yang J. L., G. L. Zhang, Y. G. Zhao, W. J. Zhao, Y. He, and X. L. Ruang. 2006. "Effect of compaction on soil water characteristics—A case study of Nanjing." *Acta Pedologica Sinica* 43(1): 33–38.

Original article posted in April 2003.

THE MYTH OF

WINTER WATERING

The Myth

"Decrease fall irrigation to force
landscape plants into winter dormancy."

Although the processes of cold hardening and dormancy development in plants are under genetic control, some people promote "assisted dormancy." The thought behind this philosophy is that we must force plants to enter dormancy or they will not be able to survive the winter. The method most commonly used to force dormancy on plants is withholding water. Many Web sites insist that you must stop watering in early fall to induce dormancy in landscape plants and turf. The rationale is that by ceasing irrigation, vegetative growth is halted, and the plant will initiate the internal processes needed to survive freezing conditions.

The Reality

To survive freezing temperatures, temperate landscape plants must become dormant and develop cold hardiness. Part of dormancy induction is the cessation of vegetative growth, during which time other biochemical and physiological changes occur. When cold temperatures finally arrive, properly hardened plants can resist freeze damage caused primarily by freeze-induced dehydration.

There is no valid reason to force dormancy on indigenous landscape plants or on plants introduced from similar climates. Temperate plants cue in on day-length changes as well as temperature differences to initiate dormancy and cold hardening. As day lengths shorten following the summer solstice, developmental processes are triggered in a species as its particular light-to-dark ratio is reached. The changes are primarily internal and are manifested outwardly as a slowing of vegetative growth and the formation of overwintering buds. While a lack of water will also cause temperate zone plants to cease vegetative growth, the presence of water will not cause these plants to grow beyond their natural period.

Decreasing irrigation of temperate landscape plants may cause more harm than good. The lack of water induces a drought stress on these plants, inhibiting their ability to undergo the biochemical and physiological changes needed to obtain maximal cold hardiness. Furthermore, the early leaf senescence induced by lack of water means the plant has fewer stored resources to put into next year's growth. The overall result will be a stunted, stress-sensitive plant.

Damage from reduced water availability also occurs below ground. Fine roots die, decreasing the ability of the plant to take up water and nutrients. Decomposition slows, and soil organisms die or move elsewhere. When dry soil freezes, it has less insulative ability than moist soil, causing the freezing and damage or death of smaller roots. The roots of landscape trees and shrubs never go dormant, and they are much less resistant to cold damage than the above-ground parts of the plant.

This myth seems to have originated from the misapplication of practices geared toward the management of summer dormant species. Such species are adapted to dry summers and cue on water availability to initiate dormancy. Many introduced ornamental bulbs, corms, and tubers are summer dormant species and need reduced irrigation to activate this process. While reducing irrigation is a valid practice for plants from arid tropical and subtropical climates, it cannot be applied to temperate woody species.

A final caveat regarding fall and winter irrigation: be sure not to overwater landscapes during this time. Poorly drained soils will lead to root injury and death due to lack of oxygen and may also promote pathogenic fungal and bacterial growth.

The Bottom Line

- Landscape plants grown in their native, or climatically similar, environments do not need dormancy forced upon them.

- The roots of landscape plants do not go dormant and are not particularly cold hardy.

- Moist soil is a better insulative barrier than dry soil.

- Management practices for summer dormant species should not be applied to winter dormant species.

❧ Managed landscapes and gardens in the Puget Sound area (and similar regions) should be kept moist, but not soggy, throughout the dormant season.

References

Anisko, T., and O. M. Lindstrom. 1996. "Survival of water-stressed *Rhododendron* subjected to freezing at fast or slow cooling rates." *HortScience* 31(3): 357–60.

Pellet, H., R. Hummel, and L. Mainquist. 1980. "Relationship of fall watering practice to winter injury of conifers." *Journal of Arboriculture* 6(6): 146–49.

Original article posted in February 2003.

WHY WEEDS WILL ALWAYS
BE IN YOUR GARDEN

Every time you weed your garden, you contribute to weed evolution. To be successful, weeds must adapt quickly to their environment, and that means adapting to the humans who would gladly pull the plug on their existence. But we aren't perfect, and when we miss a weed or two, their progeny are likely to exhibit those traits that fooled us the first time.

There are many fascinating examples of highly adaptable weeds in gardens and landscapes. One of the best known is the dandelion (*Taraxacum officinale*), the bane of those who love a perfect lawn. Consider the dandelion in a wilder situation, such as an abandoned field or other site where tall grasses and annuals dominate. The dandelions in these areas have long, floppy leaves and flowers borne on long stalks. Now compare these to dandelions found in lawns or other mown areas. Note the tight rosette of leaves and extremely short flower stalks—they are nearly nonexistent. Obviously, dandelions with long flower stalks would be mown down before they could set seed; the shorter flowers are more likely to survive the mower and produce seeds. Likewise, short tight rosettes of leaves will survive the mower better and can continue photosynthesizing. The height traits are passed down to the progeny, who will be more successful under those same environmental conditions. If conditions change, the dandelion population will shift as well.

Even more deceptive are the mimics—those weeds whose appearance and behavior allows them to lurk undetected among desirable plants. Weed mimicry has been most closely studied in crop production systems, and perhaps the most amazing example is a variety of barnyard grass (*Echinochloa crus-galli* var. *oryzicola*). Though not closely related to rice (*Oryza sativa*), *E. crus-galli* var. *oryzicola* has come to resemble this crop in both appearance and activity, especially in hand-weeded paddies. Like rice, this weed has heavy seeds that sink into the water and germinate under low levels of oxygen. The weed's growth mirrors that of the rice, always producing just a few leaves that are higher than the rice canopy and thus competing more successfully for sunlight. Once the rice (and the weed) has formed a seed head, hand weeding can begin. Yet the seed head of the weed is so fragile that it shatters on contact, spreading seeds over the paddy water, where they quickly sink and begin the cycle again. Researchers agree that these characteristics have developed in *E. crus-galli* var. *oryzicola* and other mimicking weeds through human selection activities over the past hundred years, including hand-weeding, harvesting, and seed cleaning. Through continued mistaken identity by humans, *E. crus-galli* var. *oryzicola* now more closely resembles rice than any of its own relatives.

So the next time you are silently cursing the chickweed (*Stellaria media*) that continues to hide in your blue star creeper (*Laurentia fluviatilis*), be sure to marvel at its ability to grow almost undetected before you yank it out. And rest assured that it will be back.

HOW/WHAT/WHEN/
WHERE TO PLANT

THE MYTH OF
ARBOR DAY/EARTH DAY
PLANTING IN THE WEST

The Myth

"Arbor Day/Earth Day is an ideal time to install trees."

Arbor Day, and the more recently established Earth Day, are regarded as ideal times for community volunteers to work together replanting landscapes. Arbor Day originated in Nebraska in 1872 as a way to encourage tree planting in a region largely composed of grasslands. This initial planting of one million trees was so successful that other communities in the United States and around the world adopted the practice of community tree planting in the spring. While Arbor Day is officially celebrated on the last Friday in April, actual planting dates are determined separately. Some southern states plant as early as January or February, while more northern locations may plant as late as May. These planting dates are partially based on the average date of the last hard freeze for each region. (For Washington State, Arbor Day is the second Wednesday in April.)

Earth Day, celebrated on April 22, has also been adopted as a time to revegetate human-altered landscapes. Reminiscent of the original Arbor Day, recent Earth Days have included "million-tree" planting events: "Be part of the millennium's first big tree planting campaign." As spring events, both Arbor Day and Earth Day help satisfy our urge to get outdoors and garden, clean up, or otherwise improve our environment. Planting mania is reinforced by the abundance of flowering trees and shrubs available at nurseries during the spring and summer months. One tree advocacy group's recent publication asserts, "Now [summer] is the coolest time to plant a tree!" Even though the publication later states that "trees need water," this is overridden by the directive to "choose a tree that is drought tolerant or uses a low amount of water" (reinforcing the myth that drought tolerant plants can be installed and ignored because they don't need water—a topic covered in an upcoming chapter).

The Reality

The climate in the western half of the country differs dramatically from that in the east in that summer rainfall is minimal; western regions may experience two, six, or even ten months of low rainfall. Much of the country east of the Rockies does not experience summer aridity. For example, let's compare the difference in rainfall during the months of June, July, and August. In Omaha (where Arbor Day originated), the average total precipitation during these three summer months is 10.62 inches. In Seattle, the average total is a mere 2.03 inches. This is insufficient rainfall for anything but established, native, or Mediterranean-climate plants growing under near-optimal conditions; most urban landscapes do not fall into this category.

Since the western United States experiences droughts nearly every summer, it is crucial to provide supplemental irrigation to newly installed (spring) landscapes. Generally this means a couple of hours of watering once or twice a week. Keep in mind that trees and shrubs planted in the spring and summer use a significant amount of their resources for above-ground growth. Since root growth is favored during the dormant season, it's best to install landscape plants in the fall. It has been demonstrated that shrubs and trees planted in the fall suffer less environmental stress than those planted in the spring or summer.

The Bottom Line

- Newly installed plants, even those that are drought tolerant at maturity, require substantial irrigation throughout their first season.

- Spring-planted trees and shrubs in the western United States will require substantial irrigation during their first summer.

- In moderate western climates, choose an autumn date for community planting efforts. Irrigation is less of an issue as temperatures drop and root systems begin to establish during the winter months.

- Be sure to clear any existing vegetation, especially turf, from the planting area. Mulch well after installing plants.

❧ Use Arbor Day and Earth Day as opportunities for maintaining existing landscapes. Pruning, weeding, mulching, etc., are all beneficial activities that volunteers can learn to do and that have big visual impacts.

References

Hanson, A. M., J. R. Harris, and R. Wright. 2004. "Effects of transplant season and container size on landscape establishment of *Kalmia latifolia* L." *Journal of Environmental Horticulture* 22:133–38.

Harris, J. R., J. Fanelli, and P. Thrift. 2002. "Transplant timing affects early root system regeneration of sugar maple and northern red oak." *HortScience* 37(6): 984–87.

Knight, P., and J. Fanelli. 1996. "Fall transplanting improves establishment of balled and burlapped fringe tree (*Chionanthus virginicus* L.)." *HortScience* 31(7): 1143–45.

Richardson-Calfee, L. E., and J. R. Harris. 2005. "A review of the effects of transplant timing on landscape establishment of field-grown deciduous trees in temperate climates." *HortTechnology* 15(1): 132–35.

Original article posted in October 2001.

THE MYTH OF
CLOROXED CLIPPERS

The Myth

*"A bleach solution is the best choice for
disinfecting pruning wounds and tools."*

Anyone who has made an investment in top-quality pruning
tools probably cleans and maintains them on a regular basis. But
would you clean them every day—maybe several times? If you are
worried about potentially transmitting plant diseases such as fire
blight, Dutch elm disease, and sudden oak death, then such a
cleaning regimen would be crucial. Furthermore, you might be
inspired to disinfect the pruning wounds, especially those made
on diseased trees and shrubs. The question is—what to use as
your disinfectant?

Nearly all of the popular Web sites with advice regarding tool disinfection say something like this: "Sterilize pruning tools using a solution of 1½ cups of liquid chlorine bleach in 2 gallons of water. After each cut, dip the pruner or saw into this solution before starting the next cut." This advice is repeated on thousands of Web pages, including .edu sites. Is chlorine bleach the best choice?

The Reality

I do not recommend the use of chlorine bleach as a disinfectant in gardens and landscapes for a variety of scientific and practical reasons:

1 TOOL DAMAGE. According to the MSDS (material safety data sheet) for Clorox, as well as other brands of bleach, "prolonged contact with metal may cause pitting or discoloration." Indeed, this includes your pruning tools. Bleach is an oxidizing agent, which means it is corrosive. You don't find bleach for sale in unlined metal containers, and there's a reason for that.

2 CLOTHING DAMAGE. It's pretty self-evident that bleach will, well, bleach your clothing. Any spills are impossible to treat unless you can immerse the affected material immediately. It probably is not a smart idea to carry a bottle of bleach in your pocket. And the cloths used to wipe your tools down after treatment will disintegrate quickly and have to be replaced continually.

3   HUMAN HEALTH RISK. Chlorine bleach (such as Clorox) is listed on the MSDS as an acute and chronic health hazard. In addition to the damage it can do to your clothing and tools, contact with bleach will irritate your skin—and your nose, throat, and lungs, if vapors are inhaled. Medical conditions such as asthma, chronic bronchitis, and obstructive lung disease are aggravated by exposure to chlorine bleach. Though you would most likely be in a well-ventilated area when pruning plants, to minimize health risks, you should also wear impervious gloves and safety glasses when using bleach. This means more equipment to carry.

4   PLANT HEALTH RISK. Bleach is extremely phytotoxic, more so than any of the other commonly used disinfectants. Any bleach left on your pruning tools will damage the tissue of the next cut. Likewise, pruners with reservoirs that release disinfectant as they cut should never be used.

Other disinfectant treatments include:

❧ ALCOHOL DIPS (ETHANOL OR ISOPROPYL ALCOHOL). Alcohols are readily available and moderately safe and effective to use. They can be expensive, however.

❧ ALCOHOL DIPS + FLAMING. Though this is standard procedure for tissue culture, it's not practical for outdoor use.

❧ COPPER COMPOUNDS (COPPER OXIDE, BORDEAUX MIXTURE). These are powerful fungicides and readily available. However, they probably are not the most environmentally friendly choice. There has not been a great deal of research on their effectiveness as pruning tool disinfectants.

❧ FORMALIN (HCHO). Formalin is used in embalming fluid and readily penetrates skin. Not a good choice.

❧ HOUSEHOLD CLEANERS (LISTERINE, LYSOL, PINE-SOL). These are readily available, moderately safe, and can be extremely effective. Lysol (the original, phenol-based material) in particular was found to be least corrosive to pruning tools. This is my personal choice.

❧ TRISODIUM PHOSPHATE (NA3PO4). Like bleach, this compound is corrosive and probably not a good choice for outdoor work.

Pruning tools that are regularly disinfected need to be kept in top condition. The older the blades, the more pitted they become; these pits can harbor microbes that are unaffected by quick sterilization. This is especially true of bacteria associated with active cankers; the sticky matrix is often difficult to remove from pruner surfaces. One study found that disinfectant solutions would not remove bacterial slime from the surface of cutting tools, especially if the tool surface was pitted.

Before being disinfected, tools should be cleansed of dirt and debris so that the disinfecting solution can reach every cutting surface. Disinfectant solution can be carried into the field in a tightly sealed plastic bottle; ideally this bottle should be wide enough that tools can be dipped directly into it. If this is not feasible, solution can be applied with a clean cloth or poured over the tool held over a bucket. Disinfecting solutions should not be allowed to contaminate the soil.

Finally, disinfectants should never be applied to pruning wounds, though old literature from the 1930s and 1940s often recommended this practice. This just adds insult to injury, making it more difficult for the plant to treat the wound with its own arsenal of disinfectants. Indeed, more recent research has established that pruning wounds treated with ethanol and other disinfectants had more cambial necrosis (browning of the living tissue underneath the bark) and wood discoloration than tissues left alone. Furthermore, treated wounds were inhibited from forming the callus tissue that protects damaged tissue. The only exception to this may be in treating cut stumps where regrowth is desired; in such cases sterilizing the broad, flat surface of the stump may prevent pathogen infection.

The Bottom Line

- If you are worried about transmitting plant diseases with pruning tools, then tool disinfection is warranted.

- Choose a disinfectant that is effective, readily available and affordable, relatively safe to handle, and won't harm your tools or clothing. Many household cleaners fit this description.

- Be sure to clean tools of dirt and debris before disinfecting.

- After dipping your pruning tools, be sure to wipe away excess disinfectant to avoid injuring the next plant.

- A longer soaking may be needed for pruning surfaces that are not smooth.

- Like pruners, any tools that contact internal plant tissues should always be sterilized before and after use.

⤳ Never use disinfectants directly on pruning wounds; they are phytotoxic and cause more harm than good.

References

Jullien, J. 2004. "Caring for hedgerows: The 3 P's—Planting, pruning and integrated protection." *Phytoma* 572:20–24.

Kleinhempel, H., M. Nachtigall, W. Ficke, and F. Ehrig. 1987. "Disinfection of pruning shears for the prevention of the fire blight transmission." *Acta Horticulturae* 217:211–18.

McCain, A. H., J. L. Andersen, and W. E. Welch. 1976. "Disinfectants for Dutch elm disease." *California Plant Pathology* 33:3–5.

Moutia, M., and A. Dookun. 1999. "Evaluation of surface sterilization and hot water treatments on bacterial contaminants in bud culture of sugarcane." *Experimental Agriculture* 35(3): 265–74.

Opgenorth, D. C., L. Butler, and M. Arciero. 1983. "Transmission of *Ceratocystis ulmi* on pruning saws." *Journal of Arboriculture* 9(7): 196–97.

Perry, E., and A. H. McCain. 1988. "Incidence and management of canker stain in London plane trees in Modesto, California." *Journal of Arboriculture* 14(1): 18–19.

Skimina, C. A. 1985. "Use of monochloramine as a disinfectant for pruning shears." *Combined Proceedings, International Plant Propagators' Society* 34:214–20.

Teviotdale, B. L., M. F. Wiley, and D. H. Harper. 1991. "How disinfectants compare in preventing transmission of fire blight." *California Agriculture* 45(4): 21–23.

Original article posted in January 2005.

THE MYTH OF
PROTECTIVE PRESERVATIVES

The Myth

"The chemicals in pressure-treated lumber
will not affect adjacent soils or plants."

One of the functional drawbacks of using organic materials in a landscape is the eventual disintegration of those materials through insect and microbial activity. This is especially true of lumber used for decks and raised beds, where direct contact with soil and moisture enhances its decomposition. The advent of pressure-treatment as a wood-preserving process in the early half of the last century greatly increased the functional life span of outdoor wooden structures. For many years, the chemical used to treat wood was chromated copper arsenate (CCA). Chromium locks the arsenic and copper into the wood, rendering it resistant to insects and fungi, respectively. The process was perfected by the 1960s, and by the 1970s most of the lumber used outdoors was pressure-treated with CCA.

In the last few decades, concerns have been raised as to the environmental and human health risks posed by pressure-treated lumber, especially timbers used for creating vegetable gardens. One university Q&A Web page fields the question "Are cross timbers ok for a vegetable bed?" with the answer "If by cross timbers they mean pressure treated landscape timbers or railroad ties, the answer is yes." This same article concludes that "arsenic was not leaching from timbers used in raised bed gardens varying in age from 6 months to 9 years of age." Another university Web page states that wood treated with CCA and related compounds "are the safest for the garden because of their very low tendency to leach into the soil. Research studies have shown that there is very little chance of ingesting arsenic in vegetables near treated lumber." If this is true, then why is CCA-treated lumber being phased out for residential use?

The Reality

There is no doubt that pressure-treatment with CCA works well to preserve outdoor lumber. Unfortunately, the properties that make CCA a potent, broad-spectrum pesticide also make it hazardous to humans and other nontarget organisms.

The Environmental Protection Agency (EPA) is currently assessing the risks associated with CCA-treated lumber, especially when used in children's play structures. Their Web site recommends against using CCA-treated wood "under circumstances where the preservative may become a component of food or animal feed," including as a mulch and in compost bins. In light of these cautions, it is odd that there is nothing mentioned regarding the potential risk of arsenic uptake by vegetables grown near CCA-treated timbers.

There is a significant body of recent literature that addresses the leaching and environmental uptake of chromium and arsenic from a variety of sources, including CCA-treated lumber. Space constraints preclude an in-depth review of this literature, but some of the salient points are given here:

- CCA-treated wood leaches arsenic at concentrations above the U.S. federal toxicity characteristic limit (5 mg/L).

- CCA-treated wood exposed to solar ultraviolet leaches more arsenic than unexposed wood.

- Arsenic has higher bioavailability (i.e., it can be most easily taken up by roots) in contaminated sandy soils than in contaminated clay soils.

- CCA-treated lumber is a significant nonpoint source of arsenic in suburban catchments, such as retention ponds.

- The release rates of chromium and arsenic from CCA-treated chain-saw sawdust, circular-saw sawdust, and spade-bit shavings are many times higher than those from solid wood.

- Sawdust made from CCA-treated lumber and used as a soil amendment releases high levels of chromium and arsenic into the soil.

- Significant leaching of metals from CCA-treated lumber occurs under acidic conditions.

How does this translate into vegetable gardens and food safety? Again, there is a substantial collection of recent scientific articles that address the effects of arsenic and chromium on common vegetables. While plants may tolerate growing in contaminated soils, they vary in their response to the metal. For instance, some vegetables (including beets, lettuce, onions, soybeans, and tomatoes) accumulate arsenic and/or chromium in their root tissues. Others, such as beans, leeks, and radishes, transport the metals through their roots into shoot tissues. Of most concern to me are members of the Brassicaceae (including cauliflower, kale, and cabbage), which concentrate chromium at levels far higher than that of other species, and basil and zucchini, which accumulate toxic levels of arsenic.

The most relevant of all the studies are those that combined CCA-treated lumber and/or adjacent soils with tissue analysis of plants grown in their presence. One study reported a ten-fold increase in arsenic levels in lettuce and tomatoes grown in CCA-treated raised beds, compared to those grown in beds made from untreated wood. Another study in 2004 found elevated levels of arsenic in soils adjacent to CCA-treated utility poles and fences and correlated this to enhanced arsenic accumulation in carrots and lettuce. The accumulation was magnified when phosphate was added (a ubiquitous component of most fertilizers) and could be reduced by the addition of compost, which apparently serves to bind the arsenic and prevent its uptake.

Existing CCA-treated lumber can be treated with film sealants or wrapped in heavy-duty plastics that prevent arsenic and chromium from leaching into the soil. In constructing new raised beds and other landscape structures, consider alternatives to CCA-treated lumber, including:

- naturally resistant types of wood, including cedar and juniper

- lumber treated with less toxic solutions, such as those containing copper and boron

- synthetic lumber, including lumber made from recycled plastics or rubber

- concrete blocks and other inorganic structural materials

A wood-products industry spokesman interviewed a few years ago about the hazards of CCA-treated lumber asserted, "Scientifically, there's really no data to back up any dangers. It's mostly emotionally based." This hearkens back to 1941, when a wood-products researcher stated that "treated timber is non-poisonous to warm-blooded animals," and that once it was air-dried it could "be handled with complete safety." In fact, scientific evidence demonstrates that these statements are not only inaccurate but dangerous in that they promote a false sense of security. We can only hope that industry viewpoints will catch up with reality.

The Bottom Line

- Pressure-treated lumber containing chromated copper arsenate should never be used in vegetable gardens.

- Soils that are acidic and sandy are more likely to leach heavy metals from treated lumber.

ᥲ Exposure to sunlight and other weathering activities will increase the leaching rate of CCA-treated lumber.

ᥲ Many common vegetable species accumulate arsenic and chromium in their tissues; members of the Brassicaceae may be the worst accumulators.

ᥲ Phosphate addition will enhance the ability of plants to take up arsenic and chromium.

ᥲ Addition of compost to CCA-contaminated soils may help bind arsenic and chromium, reducing uptake by plant roots.

References

Leaching of Treated Wood

Cooper, P. A., Y. T. Ung, and D. P. Kamden. 1997. "Fixation and leaching of red maple (*Acer rubrum* L.) treated with CCA-C." *Forest Products Journal* 47(2): 70–74.

Cooper, P. A., Y. T. Ung, and R. MacVicar. 1997. "Effect of water repellents on leaching of CCA from treated fence and deck units—An update." *International Research Group on Wood Preservation* (IRG/WP/97–50086): 6.

Lebow, S., R. S. Williams, and P. Lebow. 2003. "Effect of simulated rainfall and weathering on release of preservative elements from CCA treated wood." *Environmental Science and Technology* 37(18): 4077–82.

Lebow, S. T., and M. Tippie. 2001. "Guide for minimizing the effect of preservative-treated wood on sensitive environments." *Forest Products Laboratory General Technical Report*, USDA Forest Service (FPL-GTR-122): 18.

Lebow, S. T., S. A. Halverson, J. J. Morrell, and J. Simonsen. 2000. "Role of construction debris in release of copper, chromium, and arsenic from treated wood structures." *Forest Products Laboratory Research Paper,* USDA Forest Service (FPL-RP-584): 6.

Rice, K. C., K. M. Conko, and G. M. Hornberger. 2002. "Anthropogenic sources of arsenic and copper to sediments in a Suburban Lake, Northern Virginia." *Environmental Science and Technology* 36(23): 4962–67.

Stook, K., T. Tolaymat, M. Ward, B. Dubey, T. Townsend, G. H. Solo, and G. Bitton. 2005. "Relative leaching and aquatic toxicity of pressure-treated wood products using batch leaching tests." *Environmental Science and Technology* 39(1): 155–63.

Warner, J. E., and K. R. Solomon. 1990. "Acidity as a factor in leaching of copper, chromium and arsenic from CCA-treated dimension lumber." *Environmental Toxicology and Chemistry* 9(11): 1331–37.

Arsenic and Chromium Uptake by Plants

Cao, X. M., and Q. Lena. 2004. "Effects of compost and phosphate on plant arsenic accumulation from soils near pressure-treated wood." *Environmental Pollution* 132(3): 435–42.

Larsen, E. H., L. Moseholm, and M. M. Nielsen. 1992. "Atmospheric deposition of trace elements around point sources and human health risk assessment: II. Uptake of arsenic and chromium by vegetables grown near a wood preservation factory." *Science of the Total Environment* 126(3): 263–75.

Martin, R. R., A. Tomlin, and B. Marsello. 2000. "Arsenic uptake in orchard trees: Implications for dendroanalysis." *Chemosphere* 41(5): 635–37.

Mattina, M. I., W. Lannucci-Berger, C. Musante, and J. C. White. 2003. "Concurrent plant uptake of heavy metals and persistent organic pollutants from soil." *Environmental Pollution* 124(3): 375–78.

Paulraj, C., and U. S. Ramulu. 1994. "Effect of soil application of low levels of urban sewage sludge on the uptake of nutrients and yield of certain vegetables." *Journal of the Indian Society of Soil Science* 42(3): 485–87.

Peryea, F. J. 1998. "Phosphate starter fertilizer temporarily enhances soil arsenic uptake by apple trees grown under field conditions." *HortScience* 33(5): 826–29.

Rahman, F. A., D. L. Allan, C. J. Rosen, and M. J. Sadowsky. 2004. "Arsenic availability from chromated copper arsenate (CCA)-treated wood." *Journal of Environmental Quality* 33(1): 173–80.

Speir, T. W., J. A. August, and C. W. Feltham. 1992. "Assessment of the feasibility of using CCA (copper, chromium, and arsenic)-treated and boric acid-treated sawdust as soil amendments. I. Plant growth and element uptake." *Plant and Soil* 142(2): 235–48.

Warren, G. P., B. J. Alloway, N. W. Lepp, B. Singh, F. J. M. Bochereau, and C. Penny. 2003. "Field trials to assess the uptake of arsenic by vegetables from contaminated soils and soil remediation with iron oxides." *Science of the Total Environment* 31(1–3): 19–33.

Original article posted in June 2005.

THE MYTH OF
ROOT SNORKELS

The Myth

*"Low-oxygen root zones can be aerated
by installing vertical aeration tubes."*

One of the oddest and increasingly frequent landscape practices
I've seen is the incorporation of vertical plastic pipe during street
tree installation. These aeration tubes are required in some cities'
planting specs, specifically for street trees in public right-of-ways,
sidewalk planter pits, planting strips, and medians. The three- to
four-inch plastic pipes are sometimes perforated and run from
the bottom of the planting hole to the soil surface. The pipes are
left empty and uncapped, or filled with pea gravel. Proponents
claim that the tubes increase oxygen supply to the roots, allow the
evaporation of excess moisture, and can assist in efficient sum-

mer watering. In urban areas with compacted soils, proponents argue that this practice will improve street tree establishment and survival. Can root "snorkels" rescue oxygen-starved street trees?

The Reality

Aeration tubes have been used successfully and most commonly in aquatic environments, such as aquaria, hydroponic greenhouses, and waste-water treatment plants. In these systems, there is active oxygen delivery via a pump or other aerating device. In contrast, aeration pipes in soil environments are a passive transfer mechanism, where oxygen diffuses from the atmosphere into the soil surrounding the pipes.

The origin of this practice is difficult to trace. A lone study, more than twenty years old, suggested that perforated pipe was effective in oxygenating container trees. More recently, a handful of studies have investigated the use of aeration pipes in outdoor situations. Most of these have focused on phytoremediation (which uses plants to remove contaminants from soil and water) and on efforts to improve tree root growth in these suboptimal conditions. Aeration tubes were not found to be useful in improving plant growth or root development of *Populus* spp. (a genus which includes poplars and cottonwoods and is known for vigorous root growth); researchers concluded that "passive oxygen addition appeared to have little effect on root density."

The most relevant research comes from Davis, California, and focuses on usage of aeration tubes in both greenhouse and field situations. The results from the greenhouse study reported that "there is no positive effect of the pipe on ODR (oxygen diffusion rate) in the base soil." Field experiments are ongoing, but initial data echo the greenhouse study. It appears that passive aeration of root zones is not effective in anything but container trees.

A potentially useful installation technique that merits more study is the use of oxygen releasing compounds (ORCs) in poorly oxygenated soils. These compounds have been used effectively to deliver oxygen to beneficial microbes used for oil spill treatments and other forms of environmental remediation. Those earlier researchers working with *Populus* spp. found that ORCs increased root densities, while other efforts to deliver oxygen were unsuccessful. ORCs deliver oxygen not only to tree roots but to beneficial microbes needed to colonize roots as well. One-time use of ORCs might be enough of a boost to initiate root growth and increase the chances of successful tree establishment. Though not yet readily available at nurseries or other retail outlets, ORCs can be purchased on-line .

Finally, a number of gardening practices can improve soil aeration and root health. Many of these need to be implemented at the time of installation (e.g., working when the soil is dry and reducing compaction from people and equipment), and others can be instituted at any time (e.g., increasing organic mulch). Any practice that reduces soil compaction will increase aeration and drainage.

The Bottom Line

~ No scientific evidence suggests that passive aeration pipes will improve soil oxygen levels in gardens or landscapes.

~ Tree installation costs are unnecessarily increased by the installation of aeration tubes.

⤸ Chemical oxygen-releasing compounds can increase oxygen concentrations in root zones and markedly improve root growth.

⤸ Proper management of landscape soils during and after tree installation can improve gas transfer throughout the root zone and may prevent problems from developing in the first place.

References

Biran, I., and A. Eliassaf. 1980. "The effect of container size and aeration conditions on growth of roots and canopy of woody plants." *Scientia Horticulturae* 12(4): 385–94.

MacDonald, J. D., L. R. Costello, J. M. Lichter, and D. Quickert. 2004. "Fill soil effects on soil aeration and tree growth." *Journal of Arboriculture* 30(1): 19–27.

Rentz, J. A., B. Chapman, P. J. J. Alvarez, and J. L. Schnoor. 2003. "Stimulation of hybrid poplar growth in petroleum-contaminated soils through oxygen addition and soil nutrient amendments." *International Journal of Phytoremediation* 5(1): 57–72.

Original article posted in October 2003.

THE MYTH OF
VEHICULAR VIBRATION

The Myth

*"Vibration from traffic causes soil
compaction in adjacent landscapes."*

Urban soils are subjected to numerous environmental stresses. They may suffer from nutrient deficiencies, mineral toxicities, and chemical contamination. Urban soil compaction, however, may be the most significant stress, especially in terms of plant and soil health. Soil is compacted deliberately during preparation for pouring foundations and roads, and more thoughtlessly through unrestricted vehicular, human, and animal traffic. Even raindrops and irrigation spray contribute to the compaction of bare soil.

In addition to the crushing weight of construction and other vehicles, the vibration from said vehicles is often identified as another source of soil compaction. This belief has expanded to include landscapes adjacent to roadways (e.g., traffic circles and parking strips) but not directly impacted by traffic. How much does vibration contribute to soil compaction? Curious, I investigated the peer-reviewed literature to discover whether this belief was based on science or assumptions.

The Reality

Unfortunately, there is little in the scientific literature that deals directly with traffic vibration and urban landscape soils. However, there are a number of related topics from which inferences can be drawn.

First, it's clear that soil type and water content will greatly influence whether vibration will increase or decrease compaction. Sandy soils are the most porous and will settle the most when exposed to vibrations; finer-textured silt and clay soils are less likely to compact under similar conditions. Dry soils are less likely to compact than wet ones.

Second, we need to separate soil compaction due to weight from that due to vibration. Nonuniform soil compaction results from a weight applied directly to the surface of the soil (such as rainfall, feet, or tires). Weight compaction is greatest at the surface and dissipates as one goes deeper into the soil profile; compaction can extend several inches into the soil profile, depending on the weight of the compacting force and other environmental conditions. In contrast, vibrational compaction is a uniform settling of soil induced by energy waves (primarily sound) and not weight. Therefore, surface compaction is not caused by vibration from vehicles or other sources.

Many studies, unfortunately, document soil compaction by tractors and other agricultural machinery using combined weight and vibration without separating their effects. It is likely that the two forces are synergistic; that is, compaction due to the combined effect of weight and vibration is likely to be greater than the sum of the effects of weight and vibration tested separately. Industrial applications combine both weight and vibration to compact soils to the greatest possible density. Thus, vibratory rollers are commonly used to prepare roadbeds, rice fields, and in conjunction with mechanized tree planting. Such vibrational soil compaction has been especially effective in field situations where soils are coarse, nutrient-poor, and excessively well drained (i.e., relatively dry); compacting these soils has improved crop quality and yield. In contrast, crop yield was decreased in moist, coarse soils compacted by vibrating machinery. None of these studies addressed the compacting effect of vibration alone, however.

There is research evidence to support the hypothesis that vibration alone can both increase and decrease soil compaction. Vibrating probes are often used in laboratory situations to compact materials in greenhouse pots or soil columns prior to experimentation. In every case, coarse, moist soils were most easily compacted by this method. However, a number of researchers have reported on the ability of vibration processes to relieve severe compaction stress in the field, some of which were 33 percent more effective in reducing compaction than nonvibratory methods. We can probably assume that vibration will compact very loose soils and loosen very compacted ones.

A final word of practicality must be inserted here. In assessing the likelihood of vibration-induced compaction for any site, we need to remember that unlike the soils in laboratory columns and experimental fields, urban landscape and garden soils are more than just substrate. Root systems, especially those of trees and shrubs, will stabilize soils and make them less likely to shift due to vibrational disturbance. Thus, there is little reason to assume that vibration alone poses much of a danger to our landscape and garden plants.

The Bottom Line

ॐ Compaction of urban soils is caused primarily by weight applied to the soil surface, including construction equipment and other vehicles, human and animal foot traffic, and rainfall.

ॐ Moist, coarse soils are the most susceptible to compaction.

ॐ Vibration in combination with an applied surface weight will compact soils to a greater extent than weight alone.

ॐ There is no evidence that vibration alone can compact urban landscape soils.

ॐ In the absence of surface weight, soils are generally loosened when exposed to vibration.

References

Abu-Hamdeh, N. H. 2004. "The disturbance of topsoil using ultrasonic waves." *Soil and Tillage Research* 75(1): 87–92.

Gooderham, P. T. "Some aspects of soil compaction, root growth and crop yield." *Agricultural Progress* 52:33–44.

Oliviera, I. B., A. H. Demond, and A. Salehzadeh. 1996. "Packing of sands for the production of homogenous porous media." *Soil Science Society of America Journal* 60(1): 49–53.

Oussible, M., R. R. Allmaras, R. D. Wych, and R. K. Crookston. 1993. "Subsurface compaction effects on tillering and nitrogen accumulation in wheat." *Agronomy Journal* 85(3): 619–25.

Ripple, C. F., R. V. James, and J. Rubin. 1974. "Packing-induced radial particle-size segregation: Influence on hydrodynamic dispersion and water transfer measurements." *Soil Science Society of America Proceedings* 38(2): 219–22.

Saqib, G. S., M. E. Wright, and T. R. Way. 1982. "Clod size reduction by vibratory diggers." *American Society of Agricultural Engineers Paper No. 82-1546*, 16 pp.

Schack, H., and E. E. Hildebrand. 1988. "Influence of mechanical cultivation of a sandy soil on root growth of forest plants." *Allgemeine Forst und Jagdzeitung* 159(1–2): 27–34.

Sharma, P. K., K. T. Ingram, and D. Harnpichitvitaya. 1995. "Subsoil compaction to improve water use efficiency and yields of rainfed lowland rice in coarse-textured soils." *Soil and Tillage Research* 36(1–2): 33–44.

Tubeileh, A., V. Groleau-Renaud, S. Plantureux, and A. Guckert. 2003. "Effect of soil compaction on photosynthesis and carbon partitioning within a maize-soil system." *Soil and Tillage Research* 71(2): 151–61.

Original article posted in April 2006.

THE MYTH OF
XERISCAPING

The Myth

*"Use of drought-tolerant plants reduces
residential water consumption."*

When summer approaches and the prospect of water shortages
loom, many of us search for alternatives to water-hungry lawns
and annuals. In areas where arid summers are typical, the search
often leads to xeriscaping, or landscaping with drought-tolerant
trees and shrubs (xeriphytes). Not only do these landscapes survive with significantly less irrigation, but when thoughtfully exe-
cuted they harmonize with the natural landscape. It is a pleasure
to see these more environmentally appropriate landscapes replace
the turf-and-petunia gardens so prevalent in the southwestern
United States. In addition to their drought tolerance, native xeri-

phytes offer habitat to native mammals, birds, insects, and reptiles. What could possibly be wrong with this picture?

The Reality

By definition, xeriphytes are adapted to drought, but this does not mean that they don't like water. In fact, xeriphytes are particularly adept at taking up and storing water when it's available. One study demonstrated that mesquites—a staple of xeric landscapes—use more water than oaks under optimal conditions. The more water the plant stores, the more it can grow; new leaves appear and succulence increases. Many of these xeriphytic plants shift to a more energy-efficient form of photosynthesis if water is not limiting. We've all seen how well cacti and euphorbs grow in a greenhouse or home environment, but under natural conditions growth is much reduced. During the transition from moist to dry conditions, xeriphytic species often shed their leaves to reduce moisture loss, and enter dormancy. Drought-tolerant species can tolerate drought—but they grow slowly under droughty conditions and often are less aesthetically pleasing than when grown with abundant water. This phenomenon will hold true for any drought-tolerant species growing in any landscape—not just those in the arid southwestern United States.

What this means in terms of water management is that homeowners may use more water to improve the aesthetic quality of xeriphytic landscapes than they would with traditional landscapes. A study in Arizona several years ago demonstrated that homeowners understood the ecological principles behind xeriscaping, but their desire to have an aesthetically pleasing landscape translated into increased irrigation. Ironically, those homeowners most concerned about water shortages and conservation used more water than their neighbors with traditional landscapes!

For "water-wise" landscapes to be truly effective in conserving water, home gardeners and other landscape managers need to develop a different philosophy of landscape aesthetics. No plant will grow vigorously without adequate moisture, but drought-tolerant species will survive prolonged droughts. We need to be able to accept the bad—the leaf shedding and reduced growth—with the good.

The Bottom Line

∾ Any newly installed tree or shrub, drought tolerant or otherwise, requires adequate irrigation to establish a sufficient root system.

∾ Established, drought-tolerant trees and shrubs can survive with less water than less tolerant landscape plants.

∾ If water is available, many drought-tolerant species use more water than less tolerant landscape plants.

∾ A drought tolerant, water-conserving landscape is not going to grow as quickly or vigorously as the same landscape under increased irrigation.

References

Hanscom, Z., III, and I. P. Ting. 1978. "Responses of succulents to plant water stress." *Plant Physiology* 61(3): 327–30.

Huien, H., and P. Felker. 1997. "Field validation of water-use efficiency of the CAM plant *Opuntia ellisiana* in south Texas." *Journal of Arid Environments* 36(1): 133–48.

Hurd, B. H. 2006. "Water conservation and residential landscapes: Household preferences, household choices." *Journal of Agricultural and Resource Economics* 31(2): 173–92.

Hurd, B. H., R. St. Hilaire, and J. M. White. 2006. "Residential landscapes, homeowner attitudes, and water-wise choices in New Mexico." *HortTechnology* 16(2): 241–46.

Paine, T. D., C. C. Hanlon, D. R. Pittenger, D. M. Ferrin, and M. K. Malinoski. 1992. "Consequences of water and nitrogen management on growth and aesthetic quality of drought-tolerant woody landscape plants." *Journal of Environmental Horticulture* 10(2): 94–99.

Park, D. M., J. L. Cisar, G. H. Snyder, J. E. Erickson, S. H. Daroub, and K. E. Williams. 2005. "Comparison of actual and predicted water budgets from two contrasting residential landscapes in South Florida." *International Turfgrass Society Research Journal* 10:885–90.

Scheiber, S. M., E. F. Gilman, D. R. Sandrock, M. Paz, C. Wiese, and M. M. Brennan. 2008. "Postestablishment landscape performance of Florida native and exotic shrubs under irrigated and nonirrigated conditions." *HortTechnology* 18(1): 59–67.

Spinti, J. E., R. St. Hilaire, and D. VanLeeuwen. 2004. "Balancing landscape preferences and water conservation in a desert community." *HortTechnology* 14(1): 72–77.

Stabler, L. B., and C. A. Martin. 2004. "Irrigation and pruning affect growth water use efficiency of two desert-adapted shrubs." *Acta Horticulturae* 638:255–58.

Original article posted in July 2003.

HOW TO AVOID PHOSPHATE OVERLOADS
IN YOUR LANDSCAPE SOILS

Before you can address phosphate management in your landscape, you'll need a soil test to establish its baseline levels. More likely than not, your test will reveal at least adequate, if not abundant, levels of phosphate in the soil. Don't be misled by testing information that reports "available" and "unavailable" phosphorus; this refers only to plant availability. Many microbes, especially mycorrhizal fungi, can solubilize so-called unavailable phosphorus, which plants then utilize.

⚥ Reduce the use of any landscape fertilizer that contains a relatively high amount of phosphate in its formulation. This is easy to see by looking at the three digit N-P-K number on the container. The second number (phosphorus) needs to be much lower than the first number (nitrogen). The best choices are those whose P number is close to zero.

⚥ Reduce the use of any unlabelled organic material that is likely to contain high levels of phosphate. Bone meal and chicken manure are two common sources.

⚥ Don't be fooled by advertising claims that lawns need phosphate fertilizer. Recent research has led to the development of lawn fertilizers that have low, or no, phosphate. In fact, Florida now limits phosphate levels in fertilizers. See http://okeechobee.ifas.ufl.edu/News%20columns/Urban.Turf.Fertilizer.Rule.htm.

⚥ If your soils do need additional phosphate, consider rock phosphate. This low-solubility form is made available to plants gradually through microbial activity and is unlikely to cause toxicity problems or contribute to runoff pollution.

- If phosphate and other nutrient levels are higher than you would like them to be, there are ways to lower them. Increasing the soil microbe activity will help to some extent, and therefore the addition of a nutrient-poor, coarse organic mulch, such as wood chips, will draw nutrients down. Nitrogen-fixing plants, including legumes, will increase soil nitrogen levels, and this has been found to help microbes and plants tolerate higher levels of phosphate.

SOIL ADDITIVES

THE MYTH OF
EXTRAORDINARY
EPSOM SALTS

The Myth

"Adding Epsom salts to gardens is a safe,
natural way to increase plant growth."

With the increased interest in managing gardens and landscapes sustainably, products are being marketed as "safe" and "natural." Epsom salts, also known as magnesium sulfate ($MgSO_4$), are touted as "one of the most perfect nutrients for gardens and plants." Numerous claims are made to its effectiveness in increasing seed germination, improving uptake of other nutrients, and enhancing growth and overall health. "Tried and true tips" are provided, which include specific formulations for houseplants, vegetables, turf, shrubs, and trees. Dangers of nutrient overload are minimized by assurances that Epsom salts are "not persistent, so you can't overuse" them.

The Reality

The urge to use common household products as garden fertilizers and pesticides is compelling for many consumers who want simple, cheap approaches to gardening. Epsom salts have been used worldwide to relieve magnesium deficiency in commonly grown fruits (such as apples, oranges, and grapes), vegetables (including carrots, potatoes, and tomatoes), and timber species. Among these diverse plant materials that have been treated with Epsom salts are two commonalities: all are intensively produced crops, and all were suffering from magnesium deficiency. It is important to keep these two points in mind as we examine the numerous claims and recommendations regarding Epsom salts use in the garden and landscape.

Causes of Deficiency

There are two primary causes of magnesium deficiency in plants: either a lack of magnesium in the soil or an imposed deficiency caused by mineral imbalances in the soil or plant. Magnesium deficiencies most commonly occur in soils described as light, sandy, and/or acid, although occasionally clay soils under intensive production can show magnesium deficiency as well. Regardless of type, soils that are heavily leached by rainfall or irrigation are more likely to exhibit magnesium deficiency. Thus, the addition of highly soluble Epsom salts to soil under leaching conditions does not improve magnesium-deficient plants but does increase mineral contamination of water passing through the system. Less soluble sources of magnesium, such as dolomitic limestone, are preferable under these conditions.

Excessive potassium in the soil appears to interfere with root uptake of magnesium, creating a magnesium deficiency even when soil levels of magnesium are adequate. The addition of nitrogen and/or reduction of available potassium are both recommended to overcome this indirect magnesium deficiency; trees high in nitrogen were found to be less susceptible to magnesium deficiency than those with reduced nitrogen levels.

Examining the Claims

"Unlike most commercial fertilizers, which build up in the soil over time, Epsom Salt is not persistent, so you can't overuse it."

Unfortunately, this statement is incorrect. Because Epsom salts are a highly soluble form of magnesium, it is claimed that they are nonpersistent in the landscape. But several researchers have expressed concern with possible toxicities associated with excessive applications of Epsom salts. In fact, one researcher states that "magnesium residues from fertilizer unused by plants accumulate in the topsoil and are not rapidly removed by leaching."

"Spray [roses] with Epsom Salt solution weekly to discourage pests."

Epsom salts "deter pests, including slugs and voles."

There is no science to substantiate claims of pest control by Epsom salts, though the relationship has been studied since 1915, when researchers found "no apparent larvicidal effect" on flies.

Subsequent research over the decades has consistently produced negative results. Furthermore, there have been no published results of Epsom salts' efficacy against slugs or voles, and the sole published report on potential rabbit repellency was negative. Though disease control is not specifically mentioned in these claims, many popular Web sites avidly recommend Epsom salts for this purpose. Though there were two reports from the early 1960s claiming a reduction in powdery mildew on apples, no peer-reviewed articles resulted from these initial findings. A third research report found Epsom salts to have no effect upon apple scab occurrence.

"Research indicates Epsom Salt can ... help seeds germinate."

This misleading claim has no basis in scientific research. Most seeds are able to germinate in the absence of external nutrients, as they contain enough essential minerals to initiate root and shoot growth on paper towels moistened only with pure water.

"Research indicates Epsom Salt can ... make plants grow bushier."

Nebulous terms like "bushier" are difficult to quantify and are unlikely to be part of any scientific inquiry, yet I approached this claim with a great deal of latitude. Nutrient-deficient plants are less productive; thus, relieving the deficiency will improve leaf growth and return overall plant health to normal. Many scientific articles have demonstrated improved growth and production of magnesium- or sulfur-deficient plants once a usable source of the missing nutrient is supplied. Most importantly, there is no evidence that excessive levels of nutrients provided by Epsom salts or other fertilizers will cause plants to "grow bushier" or have any other measurable positive effect.

"Research indicates Epsom Salt can . . . produce more flowers."

Only two articles in my search specifically addressed flower initiation or production: one on apples, and one on orchids. The apple research was conducted on an intensively harvested crop that was known to be suffering from magnesium deficiency. It's not surprising that flowering increased once the deficiency was removed. The orchid research found no increase in flowering associated with the addition of Epsom salts, and, as another orchid researcher stated, "there is no scientific evidence that suggests the application of Epsom salts to orchids or any other plant will induce them to flower."

"Research indicates Epsom Salt can . . . increase chlorophyll production."

"Research indicates Epsom Salt can . . . improve phosphorus and nitrogen uptake."

These statements are misleading at best. Magnesium is part of the chlorophyll molecule. A deficiency of magnesium will cause a corresponding reduction in chlorophyll production (leading to the leaf chlorosis often used as an indicator of magnesium deficiency). These plants are stressed and less able to take up and utilize other nutrients, including phosphorus and nitrogen. Relieving the deficiency will improve chlorophyll production as well as nutrient uptake and usage. Any source of magnesium will accomplish this—but excessive amounts will not increase uptake beyond a plant's normal capacity.

Examining the Recommendations

"Trees: Apply 2 tablespoons per 9 square feet. Apply over the rootzone 3 times annually."

"Shrubs (evergreens, azaleas, rhododendron): 1 tablespoon per 9 square feet. Apply over root zone every 2–4 weeks."

Regardless of any claims implied by these recommendations, research has found Epsom salts to be ineffective in treating magnesium deficiency of fruit, nut, and timber tree species; slow-release magnesium sources are better choices. Research on shrubs is limited to a single article on nursery production, in which azaleas, blueberries, junipers, and hollies were grown in containers of sand and pine bark (hardly a nutrient-rich medium). A soil addition of Epsom salts improved leaf color in these magnesium-deficient plants. It would be simplistic, however, to apply these results to landscape plants. Practices that are geared toward intensive production of trees and shrubs as crops cannot be logically applied to ornamental landscapes—and there is no research on these latter situations.

"Lawns: Apply 3 pounds for every 1,250 square feet with a spreader, or dilute in water and apply with a sprayer."

An Extension circular from 1951 suggests that Epsom salts can treat fairy rings (fungal diseases) in lawns, though this recommendation was never validated scientifically. Most scientific research has focused on Epsom salts applied to highly grazed pastureland, where magnesium deficiency is a serious disorder of grazing cattle. While rapidly increasing the magnesium content of grasses, the effect is short-lived due to the highly soluble nature of Epsom salts; one study found that 49 percent of applied Epsom salts was leached from grasslands. Since we already know that overfertilized lawns contribute to water pollution, and as turfgrasses have not been shown to suffer from magnesium deficiency, it is irresponsible to recommend the indiscriminate application of Epsom salts to residential lawns.

"Roses: Add a tablespoon of Epsom Salt to each hole at planting time. Soak unplanted bushes in 1 cup of Epsom Salt per gallon of water to help roots recover. [For existing plants apply] 1 tablespoon per foot of plant height per plant; apply every two weeks. Also scratch 1/2 cup into soil at base to encourage . . . new basal cane growth."

There is no published, scientific research on Epsom salts' effect on roses. The origin of these "research-based" recommendations is unclear.

"Garden Startup: Sprinkle 1 cup per 100 square feet. Mix into soil before planting."

Unless your garden has been intensively cultivated for crop production, and/or soil tests indicate a magnesium deficiency, there is no reason to add unnecessary chemicals. No scientific research could be found to support this recommendation.

"Tomatoes: 1 tablespoon per foot of plant height per plant; apply every two weeks."

There are two relevant (though dated) reports demonstrating that a foliar application of Epsom salts can relieve magnesium deficiency of tomatoes grown in magnesium-deficient soil. No change in tomato yield was reported, however. An automatic application of Epsom salts to plants or soils that are not magnesium deficient is a poor management strategy that can injure the plants and contaminate the soil.

The Bottom Line

☙ Magnesium deficiency can occur in intensively cropped soils and in heavily grazed pasturelands.

☙ Use of Epsom salts in treating magnesium deficiency has only been studied scientifically in these specific agricultural situations.

☙ Because Epsom salts are highly soluble, a less soluble form of magnesium is recommended to treat an actual deficiency.

☙ Urban landscapes, including residential lawns and gardens, generally contain sufficient magnesium for plants.

☙ There is no scientific evidence behind the numerous claims made for applying Epsom salts to residential gardens and landscapes.

☙ It is irresponsible to advise gardeners to apply Epsom salts, or any chemical, without regard to soil conditions, plant needs, or environmental health.

References

Bolan, N. S., D. J. Horne, and L. D. Currie. 2004. "Growth and chemical composition of legume-based pasture irrigated with dairy farm effluent." *New Zealand Journal of Agricultural Research* 47(1): 85–93.

Ford, E. M., and E. L. Frick. 1962. "The effect of magnesium nutrition on the incidence of powdery mildew on potted apple rootstocks." *East Malling Research Station Annual Report* A 45:91–93.

Howard, N. F. 1937. "Magnesium sulfate valueless as a control for the bean beetle." *Science* 86(2230): 286–87.

Loganathan, P., J. A. Hanly, and L. D. Currie. 2005. "Effect of serpentine rock and its acidulated products as magnesium fertilisers for pasture, compared with magnesium oxide and Epsom salts, on a pumice soil. 2. Dissolution and estimated leaching loss of fertiliser magnesium." *New Zealand Journal of Agricultural Research* 48(4): 461–71.

Lopez, R., and E. Runkle. 2004. "The flowering of orchids: A reality check." *Orchids* 73(3): 196–203.

Majer, J. 2004. "Magnesium supply of the vineyards in the Balaton-highlands." *Acta Horticulturae* 652:175–82.

Mitchell, A. D., P. Loganathan, T. W. Payn, and R. W. Tillman. 2000. "Magnesium fertiliser dissolution rates in pumice soils under *Pinus radiata*." *Australian Journal of Soil Research* 38(3): 753–67.

Olykan, S., T. Payn, P. Beets, and M. Kimberley. 2001. "Magnesium fertilisers affected growth, upper mid-crown yellowing, and foliar nutrients of *Pinus radiata*, and soil magnesium concentration." *New Zealand Journal of Forestry Science* 31(1): 34–50.

Smith, R. C. 1937. "Magnesium sulfate—an unsatisfactory substitute for arsenicals in grasshopper baits." *Science* 86(2227): 226–28.

Wang, Y. T. 2002. "Flowering phalaenopsis: Does magnesium or phosphorus applied in the autumn promote flowering?" *Orchids* 73(8): 602–5.

Original article posted in April 2007.

THE MYTH OF
GYPSUM MAGIC

The Myth

"Adding gypsum to your yard or garden
will improve soil tilth and plant health."

Upon continued prodding from one of my university Extension colleagues, I recently watched several episodes of a well-known gardening program on television. My kids joined me, alerted by my animated responses to the host's non-stop torrent of advice. Among many amazing discoveries, I learned that by adding gypsum to my yard or garden, I would improve my problem soils by changing the particle size and loosening compaction. Further searching on the Web revealed that gypsum would also improve drainage, decrease acidity, and eliminate soil salts. Previously, I had heard of using gypsum for soil reclamation projects, but not for typical urban landscapes. Since gypsum is simply calcium sulfate, could this chemical truly transform soil structure and serve as a fertilizer for yards and gardens?

The Reality

This myth falls into the category of agricultural practices misapplied to ornamental landscapes. Gypsum effectively changes the structure and fertility of heavy clay soils, especially those that are heavily weathered or subject to intensive crop production. Gypsum also improves sodic (saline) soils by removing sodium from the soil and replacing it with calcium. Therefore, by using gypsum, one can see improvement in clay soil structure and fertility, and in desalinization of sodium-rich soils.

What other effects does gypsum have on soil and plant health? There are a number of scientific studies on gypsum usage, both in the literature and on Web sites. Briefly, researchers have found the following:

- Gypsum does not usually change soil acidity, though occasional reports of both increasing and decreasing pH exist.

- Gypsum can increase leaching of aluminum, which can detoxify soils but also contaminates watersheds.

- Gypsum can increase leaching of iron and manganese, leading to deficiencies of these nutrients.

- Gypsum applied to acid soils can induce magnesium deficiency in plants.

- Gypsum applied to sandy soils can depress phosphorus, copper, and zinc transport within the soil.

- Gypsum can have negative effects on the mycorrhizal inoculation of roots, which may account for several reports of negative effects of gypsum on tree seedling establishment and survival.

- Gypsum is variable in its effects on mature trees.

- Gypsum will not improve the fertility of acid or sandy soils.

- Gypsum will not improve the water-holding capacity of sandy soils.

- Gypsum's effects are short-lived (often a matter of months).

With the exception of arid and coastal regions (where soil salts are high) and the southeastern United States (where heavy clay soils are common), gypsum amendment is just not necessary in nonagricultural areas. Urban soils are generally amalgamations of subsoils, native and nonnative topsoils, and—in home landscapes—high levels of organic and nonorganic chemical additives. Typically, these soils are also heavily compacted and layered (and gypsum does not work well on layered soils). In such landscapes, unless you need to increase soil calcium levels, it is pointless to add yet more chemicals in the form of gypsum. Calcium deficiency can be quickly identified by any soil-testing laboratory for less than the cost of a bag of gypsum. (If you need to improve sulfur nutrition, it's wiser to use ammonium sulfate). To reduce compaction and improve aeration in nearly any landscape, application of an organic mulch is more economically and environmentally sustainable.

The Bottom Line

❧ Gypsum can improve heavy clay soil structure and remove sodium from saline soils.

❧ Gypsum has no effect on the fertility, structure, or pH of any other soil type.

❧ Most urban soils are not improved by additional gypsum.

❧ Before adding gypsum or any chemical to a landscape, have a soil analysis performed to identify mineral deficiencies, toxicities, and soil character.

❧ Adding gypsum to sandy or nonsodic soils is a waste of money, natural resources, and can have negative impacts on plant, soil, and ecosystem health.

References

Bakker, M. R., R. Kerisit, K. Verbist, and C. Nys. 1999. "Effects of liming on rhizosphere chemistry and growth of fine roots and of shoots of sessile oak (*Quercus petraea*)." *Plant and Soil* 217(1/2): 243–55.

Habte, M., and M. Soedarjo. 1995. "Mycorrhizal inoculation effect in *Acacia mangium* grown in an acid oxisol amended with gypsum." *Journal of Plant Nutrition* 18(10): 2059–73.

Harrison, W. J., D. A. MacLedo, and D. C. McKenzie. 1992. "The effect of clay addition and gypsum application on the physical properties of a hardsetting red-brown earth, and the response of irrigated cotton." *Soil and Tillage Research* 25(2/3): 231–44.

Huang, J. S., and P. V. Nelson. 2001. "Impact of pre-plant root substrate amendments on soilless substrate EC, pH, and nutrient availability." *Communications in Soil Science and Plant Analysis* 32(17–18): 2863–75.

Lopez, A., and R. Espejo. 2002. "Study of ammonium contamination in leachates from an ultisol following application of various types of amendment." *Water, Air, and Soil Pollution* 133(1): 133–43.

McCray, J. M., M. E. Sumner, D. E. Radcliffe, and R. L. Clark. 1991. "Soil Ca, Al, acidity and penetration resistance with subsoiling, lime and gypsum treatments." *Soil Use and Management* 7(4): 193–99.

Ritchey, K. D., and J. D. Snuffer. 2002. "Limestone, gypsum, and magnesium oxide influence restoration of an abandoned Appalachian pasture." *Agronomy Journal* 94:830–39.

Singh, G., J. C. Dagar, and N. T. Singh. 1997. "Growing fruit trees in highly alkali soils—a case study." *Land Degradation and Development* 8(3): 257–68

Vidal, M., A. Lopenj, R. Espejo, and R. Blazquez. 2003. "Comparative analysis of corrective action of various liming and gypsum amendments on a Palexerult." *Communications in Soil Science and Plant Analysis* 34(5–6): 709–23.

Zhu, B., and A. K. Alva. 1994. "The effect of gypsum amendment on transport of phosphorus in a sandy soil." *Water, Air, and Soil Pollution* 78(3–4): 375–82.

Original article posted in January 2004.

THE MYTH OF
PERMANENT PEATLANDS

The Myth

*"Peat moss is an environmentally friendly organic
amendment essential for many horticultural purposes."*

Peatlands are specialized types of wetlands whose value to human
civilization has been recognized for centuries. Perhaps the most
continued use of peatlands is as a fuel source: chunks of peat are
cut from bogs, dried, and used for cooking and heating purposes.
Though many societies have turned to other forms of energy production, this practice continues today, especially where other fuel
sources are absent.

Peat moss, a principal plant component of peatlands, has also
been an important part of the horticulture industry; it's used as a
soil amendment in both gardens and container plants and as an

aesthetic topdressing for potted plants and floral arrangements. Consisting primarily of *Sphagnum* species, peat moss has an amazing capacity to hold water like a sponge, slowly releasing it as the surrounding soil dries out. Since peat is 100 percent natural, it must be a truly "green" gardening product—right?

The Reality

The "greenness" of any product is determined by both its environmental impact and its method of production. Unfortunately, there is no economically realistic, environmentally friendly way to harvest peat moss. Peat is a natural resource that accumulates at the glacially slow rate of 0.5 to 1.0 millimeter per year, or about 1/25th of an inch. Peat harvesting involves the removal of deep layers of peat that have literally taken centuries to accumulate. In fact, since the term "harvesting" implies sustainability, it is more accurate to describe commercial peat removal as "mining."

To make an informed decision about whether or not to use peat moss, gardeners need to understand the roles peatlands play in the environment. Like other wetlands, peatlands are systems that help purify and store water. Perhaps most important is that they are the single largest terrestrial store of carbon, equivalent to 75 percent of all carbon in the atmosphere. Paradoxically, the destruction of peatlands is not yet recognized as a significant part of global climate change.

Most damaging to educational efforts regarding peatland conservation are industry assertions that there are no horticultural substitutes for peat moss. There is a widely held perception that this natural resource cannot be diminished; the sales material from one local peat producer claims that their supply of peat from a 150-acre lake is "virtually limitless." One industry group asserts that "peat is still the only affordable and readily available substrate that can be used to grow all kinds of plants. . . . It is still the underpinning of the horticulture industry, worldwide." Many peat moss producers focus on the restoration of peat bogs, with little, if any, mention of viable alternatives to their product.

Peatland Restoration

Degraded peatlands do not retain their former function; the changes in hydrology and physical structure are hostile to *Sphagnum* reestablishment. When degraded peatlands are restored, their ability to hold water is improved, but CO_2 continues to be released by high levels of bacterial respiration, caused by the decomposition of mulch and other organic matter. It takes a number of years for the photosynthetic rate of new peatland plants to outpace bacterial respiration; until this happens, even restored peatlands represent a net loss of carbon to the atmosphere and thus contribute to greenhouse gas production.

Peat Moss Alternatives

While efforts to restore degraded peatlands are admirable, it is more environmentally and economically sound to reduce luxury use of peat and promote viable alternatives. Contrary to what some peat moss producers claim, there are many economically feasible, environmentally sustainable substitutes for horticultural peat. International research on peat alternatives dates back at least thirty years and has identified a plethora of materials whose easy availability, low cost, and sustainability make them attractive substitutes for peat moss. These materials, alone or in combination, range from traditional materials such as composted bark, yard and agricultural wastes, and livestock manures to more current waste products, including brewing waste, coconut coir, olive mill waste, pulp and paper sludge, municipal solid waste and sewage sludge, and even foam cubes. These materials have been used in the rooting and production of many plants, including vegetables, annual flowers, houseplants, woody ornamentals, and timber species.

Granted, there have been initial problems with some of these materials, including high levels of heavy metals or salts, and too high a carbon-to-nitrogen ratio. Research continues to address these problems, refining the methods needed to produce high-quality alternatives. In fact, many of these alternative substrates have repeatedly performed better than peat in terms of plant vigor and quality. If this isn't enough of an incentive to switch to peat alternatives, consider these other documented benefits:

- It is more economically sustainable to use locally produced materials.

- Reuse of agricultural and timber waste products keeps them out of landfills.

- Fertilizer applications can be decreased by using a more nutrient-rich medium.

- Transplants are more drought-resistant when grown in media with less water-holding capacity than peat moss.

Peatland Conservation

In 1971 the Ramsar Convention on Wetlands was established in response to public concern over the increasing degradation of wetlands, including peatlands. In 2002, the convention created a committee "to monitor and guide global action for peatland management." Two of the committee's recommendations are:

- ❧ "Citizens should be provided with information and educational materials that will enable them to make informed choices concerning lifestyle and consumer behavior compatible with the wise use of peatlands."

- ❧ "Research into, and development of, appropriate sustainable alternatives to peat in, for example, horticultural use, should be encouraged."

The Ramsar Convention and its affiliated groups do not promote a hands-off approach to peatlands, but rather encourage the sustainable use of peatlands, balancing natural resource conservation and carbon protection with economic needs.

Some countries have more quickly responded to the global crisis of degraded peatlands. In the United Kingdom, for example, much of the peat extraction for horticultural purposes has been reduced or eliminated. The Peat Producers' Association in the United Kingdom and the mushroom industry (the second-largest user of horticultural peat) have commissioned research on peat alternatives and have developed peat-free products. Many UK Web sites, including that of the Royal Botanical Gardens at Kew, carry information on peat alternatives.

Finally, some countries, such as South Africa, have neither peatlands nor resources to import peat moss. These countries have managed to find suitable substitutes for horticultural peat moss and have sustainable plant production industries. To suggest that these substitutes do not exist is deceptive; to destroy a natural resource for luxury consumption is unconscionable.

The Bottom Line

❧ Peatlands are biodiverse ecosystems with important environmental functions in water purification and carbon storage.

❧ Peat moss is a nonrenewable resource whose replacement takes centuries.

❧ Degraded peatlands are ecologically non-functional, resulting increased water loss, poorer water quality, and decreased storage of atmospheric carbon.

❧ Newly restored peatlands are partially functional, as they can reduce water loss, but they contribute even more to global CO2 production than degraded peatlands.

❧ Horticultural peat moss use can be reduced and/or replaced by using a number of available materials that are both economically feasible and environmentally friendly.

❧ Consumers need to be fully informed as to the environmental function of peatlands as well as alternatives to horticultural peat moss.

References

Arenas, M., C. S. Vavrina, J. A. Cornell, E. A. Hanlon, and G. J. Hochmuth. 2002. "Coir as an alternative to peat in media for tomato transplant production." *HortScience* 37(2): 309–12.

Ball, A. S., D. Shah, and C. F. Wheatley. 2000. "Assessment of the potential of a novel newspaper/horse manure-based compost." *Bioresource Technology* 73(2): 163–67.

CC-GAP. 2005. "Peatlands. Do You Care?" Coordinating Committee for Global Action on Peatlands (CC-GAP). http://www.imcg.net/docum/Peat_ccgap.pdf. Accessed April 28, 2009.

Chen, J., D. B. McConnell, C. A. Robinson, Y. Huang, and R. D. Caldwell. 2001. "Waste compost-formulated container media for rooting and producing tropical foliage plants." *Hortscience* 36(3): 540.

Evans, M. R. 2004. "Processed poultry feather fiber as an alternative to peat in greenhouse crops substrates." *HortTechnology* 14(2): 176–79.

Garcia-Gomez, A., M. P. Bernal, and A. Roig. 2002. "Growth of ornamental plants in two composts prepared from agroindustrial wastes." *Bioresource Technology* 83(2): 81–87.

Gruda, N., and W. H. Schnitzler. 2004. "Suitability of wood fiber substrates for production of vegetable transplants. II. The effect of wood fiber substrates and their volume weights on the growth of tomato transplants." *Scientia Horticulturae* 100(1–4): 333–40.

Guerin, V., F. Lemaire, O. Marfa, R. Caceres, and F. Giuffrida. 2001. "Growth of *Viburnum tinus* in peat-based and peat-substitute growing media." *Scientia Horticulturae* 89(2): 129–42.

Ramsar Convention on Wetlands. http://www.ramsar.org/. Accessed April 28, 2009.

Shaw, N., and D. Cantliffe. 2003. "Hydroponic Beit Alpha cucumber production using pine bark as an alternative soilless media." *Hortscience* 38(5): 720.

Weider, K., and D. Vitt. "Peatland Literature." http://www.peat-net.siu.edu/Literature%20Files/BP__A-G%20Lit%20 listings.htm. Accessed April 28, 2009.

Wilson, S. B., P. J. Stoffella, and D. A. Graetz. 2003. "Compost amended media and irrigation system influence container-ized perennial *Salvia*." *Journal of the American Society for Horticultural Science* 128(2): 260–68.

Original article posted in July 2006.

THE MYTH OF
WONDROUS WATER CRYSTALS

The Myth

*"Super-absorbent water crystals will reduce your
work and help keep your plants healthy."*

The use of polyacrylamide (PAM) hydrogels, more popularly
known as "water crystals," has migrated far beyond the original
agricultural application. The ability of these synthetic polymers
to absorb water and selectively bind to other substances has led to
their use as soil stabilizers, water purifiers, juice clarifiers, animal
feed thickeners, and as agents in the processing of oil, pulp and
paper, and fruits and vegetables. Industrially, they are widely
used in making cosmetics and other personal products, and have

medical application in tissue augmentation. But people are probably most familiar with hydrogels sold as amendments for garden soils or for household use in flower arrangements, crafts, and decorations. Polyacrylamides are advertised as being "totally safe" for people and "non-toxic and safe to the environment" and can be found for sale on thousands of Web sites.

The Reality

The polyacrylamides used in gardens, landscapes, and nurseries are cross-linked polymers that form a gel when water is added (as opposed to linear polymers, which dissolve in water). Swollen to many times their original size, these gels slowly release water to the soil as they dry. Unfortunately, on-the-ground conditions can prevent PAM hydrogels from functioning optimally. Fertilizers and other dissolved substances can interfere with hydrogel water-holding capacity. Hot, dry weather conditions can lead to increased degradation and decreased effectiveness of PAM hydrogels. And for every success story, one can find a situation in which hydrogels have failed to function. Though I've previously written on this topic in *The Informed Gardener*, the ubiquitousness of PAM hydrogels in our lives, combined with their known and potential hazards, demands that we continue to question their use.

Hydrogel Effects on Plants

The documented impacts of PAM hydrogels on plant survival and establishment are variable. Some researchers report enhanced growth of crop and tree species, presumably due to improved soil water conditions. Other research, however, does not find that

PAM improves plant survival compared to control or other treatments, especially if performance is evaluated over time. In fact, several studies found that PAM-treated plants perform worse than the untreated controls and/or suffer from nutrient deficiencies.

Why is there such high variability among research results? I believe that the cause is both environmental and temporal. Many of the positive results are drawn from studies that are short-term and/or performed under controlled conditions; for instance, one study reports on tree survival only a few months after installation. As I explained in the first volume of *The Informed Gardener*, PAM gels lose their water-holding effectiveness in a relatively short period of time, especially when exposed to high levels of UV, salts, and freeze-thaw cycles. Positive results in the short term may be perfectly valid for nursery plant production, where environmental conditions can be more tightly controlled, but they are less applicable to ornamental landscapes and gardens. Indeed, it is under natural conditions over the long term that PAM gels perform most poorly.

Long-term Effectiveness

Polyacrylamides are organic chemicals that can be degraded by microbial activity as well as by environmental conditions. A number of naturally occurring soil bacteria and fungi have been identified as active decomposers of polyacrylamide gels. It's not surprising that polyacrylamide is rapidly broken down by decomposers; these gels contain a significant amount of nitrogen, which is often limited in the environment. And even if gels are somehow protected from microbial degradation, they will still be broken down by environmental factors. Exposure to ultraviolet radiation, chemicals, fertilizers, abrasion by wind or machinery, and freezing temperatures will break the polymer into smaller fragments that lack the ability to hold water. In most outdoor applications, therefore, the functional life of polyacrylamides can be as short as eighteen months; we should have serious reservations about using PAM gels in the landscape and expecting long-term results.

Polyacrylamide Gels and Human Health

There are three separate, but related, human health issues relevant to usage of PAM hydrogels: exposure to acrylamide, polyacrylamide, and polyacrylamide degradation products. Acrylamide is the structural unit (called a "monomer"; many units make a "polymer") used to synthesize polyacrylamides, and a certain percentage of free acrylamide remains in the finished product. By law, only 500 parts per million of free acrylamide is allowed in hydrogels manufactured for agricultural, garden, and household use. However, this is 100 to 500 times more than what is recommended for PAM-based cosmetics, as acrylamide is known to be neurotoxic and may be carcinogenic as well. Even so, infrequent users of garden hydrogels will probably not experience any significant exposure to acrylamide from this source.

While intact PAM gels are much less toxic than acrylamide, chronic exposure to them can cause minor problems, such as skin irritation and mucus membrane inflammation, and other, more toxic, effects associated with gels injected during plastic or cosmetic surgery. As the intact gels break down, the resulting fragments pose as yet unknown health risks. Anyone who routinely handles soilless media containing hydrogels (commonly found in container plants) will be exposed to both intact and degrading polyacrylamide.

Should you be concerned about your exposure to PAM hydrogels? This is where the big picture regarding hydrogel usage becomes important. Because these compounds are so ubiquitous, it's likely that most of us are exposed to a number of PAM gel sources every day. Studies that estimate the lifetime risks of developing cancer usually focus on only one source of exposure, such as that from usage of personal care products that contain polyacrylamide. While these individual estimates are almost always low, there have not been analyses to determine additive risks associated with exposure to multiple sources of polyacrylamide. The lack of scientific data makes it difficult to predict risks associated with exposure to polyacrylamide gels.

Hydrogels and Environmental Health

As a neurotoxin and carcinogen, acrylamide is dangerous not only to humans but to other organisms as well; the evidence does not need to be repeated here. Of greater concern for gardeners should be the impact of PAM hydrogels on other organisms in the environment.

While microbes do not appear to be negatively affected by PAM gels, and in fact degrade them vigorously, we know little about the effects on other terrestrial organisms. However, some inhabitants of aquatic systems have been studied in relation to PAM gel toxicity, and the news is not good. Cationic PAM gels, which are positively charged polymers, are attracted to the hemoglobin in fish gills, where the gel binds and suffocates the fish. A variety of algal and invertebrate species are also injured or killed when exposed to low levels of cationic PAMs, which may also contain higher levels of acrylamide monomer. Due to these deadly attributes, the use of cationic PAM gels is illegal in a number of municipalities where aquatic contamination is likely. (Information on the charged nature of any polyacrylamide product is available from its manufacturer or distributor.)

Alternative Products and Strategies

The recognized hazards associated with cationic PAM gels, as well as those associated with residual acrylamide, have spurred many researchers to develop alternatives, including resins, papermaking by-products, and a number of polysaccharides, such as gums and starches. These alternatives are more environmentally sound than polyacrylamide gels, and often cheaper to use and functionally superior as well.

The best news for those of us managing a home garden or landscape is that simple changes in management practices are often better than using any hydrogel at all. In several studies, alternative water management strategies had higher success rates than usage of PAM gels. These strategies were as simple as adding two liters of water when planting *Pinus patula* seedlings, or providing wind protection to reduce water stress in musk melon. More commonly, mulches (especially organic mulches) were rated as being superior to hydrogels in terms of erosion control, enhancing water infiltration and conservation, plant growth and establishment, and nutrient value.

The Bottom Line

❧ The useful lifespan of cross-linked PAM hydrogels used outdoors can be as short as eighteen months and at best only a few years; hydrogels cannot be regarded as long-term solutions to landscape water needs.

❧ As PAM gels degrade, they become less useful and pose unknown risks to people and ecosystems. Be aware of your total exposure to polyacrylamides from all sources, including occupational use, garden products, and cosmetics.

❧ Cationic PAM hydrogels should never be used in gardens and landscapes, as they are toxic to aquatic organisms and risky to human health.

❧ Many of the products labeled "water gel crystals" and "poly-clear" are cationic PAM gels—especially those manufactured outside the United States. If you must use PAM gels, insist on material safety data sheets to ensure that you are not purchasing cationic gels.

❧ Cultural practices that conserve soil moisture are simple, inexpensive, safe, effective, and natural alternatives to PAM hydrogels.

References

(updates in addition to those in *The Informed Gardener*)

Reviews

Chalker-Scott, L. 2008. "The Myth of Polyacrylamide Hydrogels." In *The Informed Gardener*, 124–30. Seattle: University of Washington Press.

Chalker-Scott, L. 2008. "The Myth of Polyacrylamide Hydrogels Revisited." *The Informed Gardener*, 131–36. Seattle: University of Washington Press.

Chalker-Scott, L. 2007. "Super-absorbent water crystals—Are they really so 'super?'" *MasterGardener* 1(4): 35–38.

Polyacrylamide Hydrogel Effects on Plants

Al-Humaid, A. I., and A. E. Moftah. 2007. "Effects of hydrophilic polymer on the survival of buttonwood seedlings grown under drought stress." *Journal of Plant Nutrition* 30(1–3): 53–66.

Frantz, J. M., J. C. Locke, D. S. Pitchay, and C. R. Krause. 2005. "Actual performance versus theoretical advantages of poly-acrylamide hydrogel throughout bedding plant production." *HortScience* 40(7): 2040–46.

Newhall, R. L., T. A. Monaco, W. H. Horton, R. D. Harrison, and R. J. Page. 2004. "Rehabilitating salt-desert ecosystems following wildfire and wind erosion." *Rangelands* 26(1): 3–7.

Sarvas, M. 2003. "Effect of desiccation on the root system of Norway spruce (*Picea abies* [L.] Karst.) seedlings and a pos-sibility of using hydrogel Stockosorb® for its protection." *Journal of Forest Science* 49(11): 531–36.

Syvertsen, J. P., and J. M. Dunlop. 2004. "Hydrophilic gel amendments to sand soil can increase growth and nitrogen uptake efficiency of citrus seedlings." *HortScience* 39(2): 267–71.

Youssef, E. M. A. 2003. "Influence of hydrogels compounds on acclimatization behavior of *Acacia melanoxylon* R. Br. vitro-plants." *Acta Horticulturae* 608:81–84.

Natural Degradation of Polyacrylamide Hydrogels

Ashour, I. A., M. H. Ali, F. A. Hashem, and A. Sayed. 2004. "Effect of biodegradation of some soil conditioners on soil properties under saline water conditions." *Annals of Agricultural Science, Moshtohor* 42(1): 401–13.

Sojka, R. E., J. A. Entry, and J. J. Fuhrmann. 2006. "The influence of high application rates of polyacrylamide on microbial metabolic potential in an agricultural soil." *Applied Soil Ecology* 32(2): 243–52.

Wolter, M., C. I. D. Wiesche, F. Zadrazil, S. Hey, J. Haselbach, and E. Schnug. 2002. "Biological degradability of synthetic superabsorbent soil conditioners." *Landbauforschung Volkenrode* 52(1): 43–52.

Polyacrylamide and Acrylamide Effects on Human Health

Anonymous. 2005. "Amended final report on the safety assessment of polyacrylamide and acrylamide residues in cosmetics." *International Journal of Toxicology* 24(S2): 21–50.

de Rosemond, S. J. C., and K. Liber. 2004. "Wastewater treatment polymers identified as the toxic component of a diamond mine effluent." *Environmental Toxicology and Chemistry* 23(9): 2234–42.

van Landingham, C. B., G. A. Lawrence, and A. M. Shipp. 2004. "Estimates of lifetime-absorbed daily doses from the use of personal-care products containing polyacrylamide: A Monte Carlo analysis." *Risk Analysis* 24(3): 603–19.

Xi, T. F., C. X. Fan, X. M. Feng, Z. Y. Wan, C. R. Wang, and L. L. Chou. 2006. "Cytotoxity and altered c-myc gene expression by medical polyacrylamide hydrogel." *Journal of Biomedical Materials Research A.* 78(2): 283–90.

Alternatives to Polyacrylamide Gels

Li, J. F., Z. Q. Song, and H. Gao. 2006. "Performance of sulfonated amino-formaldehyde resins on improving structure of aeolian sandy soil." *Chemistry and Industry of Forest Products* 26(3): 17–22.

Sojka, R. E., J. A. Entry, W. J. Orts, D. W. Morishita, C. W. Ross, and D. J. Horne. 2005. "Synthetic- and bio-polymer use for runoff water quality management in irrigated agriculture." *Water Science and Technology* 51(3/4): 107–15.

Yoshimura, T., R. Yoshimura, C. Seki, and R. Fujioka. 2006. "Synthesis and characterization of biodegradable hydrogels based on starch and succinic anhydride." *Carbohydrate Polymers* 64(2): 345–49.

Original article posted in October 2007.

THE MYTH OF
FISH-FRIENDLY
SOIL AMENDMENTS

The Myth

"Amending your soil with organic matter
will improve water quality in streams."

As the title of this chapter suggests, the myths surrounding the
amendment of soil prior to woody plant installation are vast and
firmly rooted. Soil amendment recommendations are found in
the "building healthy soil" genre of popular literature and consist
of sweeping generalizations regarding the benefits and uses of
organic soil amendments. One of the purported benefits of soil
amendment is " . . . storing fertilizers and natural nutrients for
gradual release, while preventing them from washing into
streams." Soil amendment is claimed to create "salmon-friendly

soils," and lengthy documents are available that calculate fluff factors and finished grades for amendment. It all appears to be very scientific and logical.

The Reality

Once again, this is a case of misapplying traditional, production-oriented agricultural practices to a permanent, ornamental landscape. Organic amendment of intensively managed agricultural soils is needed to replenish nutrients and improve soil structure. Such soils are adapted to annual disturbances, and the plant material in question is harvested yearly. The same is certainly not true of permanent installations such as ornamental landscapes.

As I've discussed in *The Informed Gardener*, many undesirable things happen to permanent landscapes when soils are liberally amended with organic matter (OM). (To be clear, we will define "amendment" as working organic matter into the soil, rather than applying it as a topdressing or mulch.) Water and air movement is restricted between the native and amended soils, and this barrier, in concert with the eventual subsidence of the soil, causes plant health to suffer.

The "salmon-friendly" claim, however, falls into another category that needs to be addressed. Organic matter is fertilizer and is composed of the same elements that make up commercial fertilizers; the primary difference is that organic matter provides a slow release of nutrients through microbial decomposition. Decades of research has established that ideal soils for plant growth contain 5 to 10 percent OM. A heavily amended topsoil (e.g., 33 percent OM) releases much greater amounts of nitrogen, phosphorus, and other nutrients than an ideal soil. When organic matter is applied in excess—that is, at levels greater than occurs

```
FERTILIZER:

* Because your soil nitrate level is very high, it may be inadvisable
to fertilize at this time. Call the lab for more information.

The organic matter level of this soil appears to be quite high. When
properly fertilized and provided proper drainage it should provide a
good growing medium for woody ornamentals which prefer a humus rich soil.

* Potassium level is very high in this soil. DO NOT   add
additional K at this time.

DO NOT FERTILIZE this soil.


-------------------------------------------------------------------
   SOIL pH    5.9       NITROGEN: NO3-N = 110 ppm        NH4-N =    5 ppm
   BUFFER pH  6.5       ORGANIC MATTER: 21.8 % (Desirable range  4-10%)

NUTRIENT LEVELS: PPM |    Low   Medium        High           Very High
Phosphorus  (P)   38 |XXXXXXXXXXXXXXXXXXXXXXXXXXXXXXXXXXXXXXXXXXXXXXXXXXXX
Potassium   (K)  430 |XXXXXXXXXXXXXXXXXXXXXXXXXXXXXXXXXXXXXXXXXXXXXXXXXX
Calcium     (Ca) 2463|XXXXXXXXXXXXXXXXXXXXXXXXXXXXXXXXXXXXXXXXXXXXXXXXXXXX
Magnesium   (Mg)  327|XXXXXXXXXXXXXXXXXXXXXXXXXXXXXXXXXXXXXXXXXXXXXXXXXX
```

FIGURE 2.

Soil test from a 100% organic garden shows excessive
nutrient loading due to high OM content (21.8%).

naturally in the soil—it will cause pollution problems just as
surely as commercial fertilizers do.

Figure 2 is an example of a soil test depicting the unfortunate
results of overamending with organic material. I've circled three
of the important points to note here. The organic matter level of
21.8 percent is significantly greater than what is recommended
and has led to the high nutrient loading of phosphorus and other
nutrients. As a result, the report strongly warns "DO NOT FER-
TILIZE this soil." The irony is that this soil test was taken from
an organic garden that demonstrates sustainable techniques.

The root zones of newly planted trees and shrubs, if installed
properly, are only a few inches deep. Any OM below this zone is
unavailable to the roots and can leach into nearby aquatic sys-

tems. The practice of soil amendment is especially irresponsible when used in restoration of habitats near streams and other bodies of water. These terrestrial systems are rarely nutrient deficient, and the addition of high nutrient loads via organic amendment will result in increased water pollution.

There is a solid body of scientific research behind the issue of organic amendment contamination of aquatic systems. Most of this comes from crop production literature, but the concepts also apply to urban landscapes that are (improperly) managed like crop fields. Several recent studies have shown that:

~ Compost phosphate is highly soluble and elevates phosphate levels in aquatic systems.

~ Ground water quality is negatively affected by high nitrogen and salt levels during compost weathering.

~ Ammonium, potassium, phosphate, and sodium create surface water pollution during manure composting.

~ Soil amendment with large amounts of manure leads to water contamination.

~ Nonpoint pollution of water resources by nitrate is caused by a combination of factors, including tillage and the amount of organic matter in the soil.

In the words of one author, "manures and fertilizers are applied to agricultural lands in excess of recommended amounts, resulting in widespread pollution of surface and ground water" (Ogg 1999). One can argue that urban landscapes and restoration sites are not agricultural lands but when these urban landscape soils are managed like agricultural soils, then the same problems occur. Instead, organic matter should be added to urban landscapes as a mulch to support tree and shrub growth.

The Bottom Line

৯ Amended landscape soils that contain more than 10 percent organic matter will also contain excessive levels of nutrients.

৯ Any soluble nutrients not immediately utilized by microbes or plants contribute to nonpoint source pollution.

৯ Before adding any organic or inorganic fertilizer to a landscape, have a soil test performed to identify nutrient deficiencies.

৯ Organic matter should be added as a mulch to permanent landscapes to provide nutrients in a more sustainable manner.

References

Chalker-Scott, L. 2008. "The Myth of Soil Amendments, Part 1." In *The Informed Gardener*, 99–102. Seattle: University of Washington Press.

Chalker-Scott, L. 2008. "The Myth of Soil Amendments, Part 2." In *The Informed Gardener*, 103–6. Seattle: University of Washington Press.

Chalker-Scott, L. 2008. "The Myth of Soil Amendments, Part 3."
    In *The Informed Gardener*, 107–10. Seattle: University of
    Washington Press.
Ogg, C. 1999. "Benefits from managing farm produced nutri-
    ents." *Journal of the American Water Resources Association*
    35(5): 1015–21.

Original article posted in December 2004.

TIPS FOR CREATING AND MAINTAINING
HEALTHY LANDSCAPE SOILS

- Try to work soil only when it's dry—it doesn't compact as easily as wet soil.

- Bare soil is unnatural and unhealthy. Although it may look neat and tidy, it experiences dramatic shifts in temperature and moisture content, erodes quickly, and becomes compacted. Embrace a less manicured look and add mulch.

- Keep all soil covered with a mixture of plant materials (especially ground covers), coarse organic or inorganic mulch, and solid surfaces (such as pavers). Diversity in soil cover is not only healthy but can be aesthetically striking as well.

- Think of soil nutrition as "slow food": use layers of compost and wood chips as nutrient sources rather than quick fixes of commercial plant fertilizers.

- Avoid using pesticides on your soils, especially fungicides—they kill friends as well as enemies. Your plant roots need a healthy colony of beneficial fungi and bacteria.

- Use a variety of plant materials in your landscape—trees, shrubs, groundcovers, perennials, bulbs, and annuals. Plant diversity will create a stable soil environment physically, chemically, and biologically.

- It's easier to prevent soil compaction than it is to fix it. Before you bring heavy equipment onto your landscape, prevent damage by covering unprotected soil or ground covers with a very thick (8" minimum) layer of coarse wood chips. After work is completed, the chips can be moved away and soils and ground covers will recover more quickly than if they had been left bare.

If your soils are compacted, don't despair: over time, they will recover. To facilitate natural recovery, keep a thick layer of coarse organic mulch over the soil. Be sure to water the area occasionally. The combination of soil surface protection, along with natural underground activity from plant roots and animals, will enhance water percolation, aeration, and recovery.

MULCHES

THE MYTH OF
ALLELOPATHIC WOOD CHIPS

The Myth

"Wood chips made from cedars will kill landscape plants."

I have an ongoing love affair with wood-chip mulches. Invariably after giving a presentation on sustainable landscape management, I get the "But what about . . . ?" questions. Recently, the concerns have been "But what about cedar wood chips? I've heard they are toxic and will kill my plants." There are many references to this ability, called allelopathy—the suppression of plant growth due to toxic compounds in the tissues of another plant— on the Internet and in popular publications. A recent article in *Grounds Maintenance* states that "allelopathic mulches include uncomposted sawdust of redwood (*Sequoia*) and cedar (*Cedrus*); the bark of spruce (*Picea*), larch (*Larix*) and Douglas fir (*Pseu-*

dotsuga); and both the leaves and sawdust of *Eucalyptus.*" Web sites warn against the use of cedar wood chips, citing cases in which toxic leachate from wood and foliage has killed plants and animals in both terrestrial and aquatic systems. Other sites suggest that volatile chemicals released from cedar foliage will inhibit seed germination, kill seedlings, and cause tip burn on the foliage of established plants. Gardening Q&A pages zoom in on the mention of cedar mulch and attribute landscape problems to its use. No wonder there is widespread concern on how safe cedar-based mulches are for healthy landscape plants.

The Reality

There are bona fide examples of allelopathy in tree species. Probably the best known is black walnut (*Juglans nigra*), which contains the compound juglone. This water-soluble member of the quinone family is found in all parts of the black walnut and is quite effective in killing competitors, especially seedlings and other shallowly rooted plants. It appears that juglone reduces oxygen uptake and photosynthetic activity, inhibiting the growth of sensitive plants. Nevertheless, there are a variety of landscape plant materials that are resistant to juglone toxicity.

On the other hand, there is virtually no documented evidence for allelopathic activity in those trees commonly called cedars (and which include *Thuja*, *Juniperus*, and *Cedrus* spp.). Though one study suggests that Douglas fir seedlings might be sensitive to *Thuja* extracts, these seedlings were held under highly artificial laboratory conditions (i.e., were submersed in solutions for seventy-four hours).

Cedars, especially *Thuja* species, have developed chemical weapons against a number of pests and pathogens. Researchers have found that *Thuja plicata* heartwood contains thujaplicin, a water-soluble tropolone that inhibits not only various bacteria and fungi but tumor activity as well. This antimicrobial activity is probably responsible for the rot-resistant nature of cedar wood. There is, however, no evidence that this substance harms plant tissues.

Another weapon in cedar's chemical arsenal is thujone, one of several essential oils found in the foliage of *Thuja* and other species, including junipers and sage. Best known for its ability to repel clothing moths, thujone and other foliar terpenes also repel, inhibit, or kill cockroaches, termites, carpet beetles, Argentine ants, and odorous house ants. These compounds are not readily soluble in water but volatilize and become airborne. The lack of solubility also suggests that this compound will not leach into nearby aquatic areas, despite concerns to the contrary.

The Bottom Line

~ It is unlikely that wood-chip mulches containing cedar will have negative effects on established landscape plants.

~ The allelopathic activities attributed to mulches made from cedar and other species may actually be due to other factors, such as nutrient and light limitations.

~ Seeds and seedlings, whether weeds or desirable species, are more sensitive to mulch suppression, as they do not have established root systems.

References

Anderson, J. T., H. G. Thorvilson, and S. A. Russell. 2002. "Landscape materials as repellents of red imported fire ants." *Southwest Entomologist* 27:155–63.

Carlson, C. R. "Mulching basics: Are you covered?" *Grounds Maintenance*. http://grounds-mag.com/mag/grounds__maintenance__mulching__basics__covered/index.html. Accessed February 2, 2009.

Chalker-Scott, L. 2007. "Arborist wood chip mulches—Landscape boon or bane?" *MasterGardener* 1(3): 21–23.

Chalker-Scott, L. 2007. "Impact of mulches on landscape plants and the environment—A review." *Journal of Environmental Horticulture* 25(4): 239–49.

Duryea, M. L., R. J. English, and L. A. Hermansen. 1999. "A comparison of landscape mulches: Chemical, allelopathic, and decomposition properties." *Journal of Arboriculture* 25:88–96.

Harris, R. W., J. R. Clark, and N. P. Matheny. 2004. *Arboriculture: Integrated Management of Landscape Trees, Shrubs, and Vines*. 4th ed. Upper Saddle River, NJ: Prentice Hall.

Original article posted in June 2003.

THE MYTH OF
NITROGEN-NABBING
WOOD CHIPS

The Myth

*"Wood-chip mulches tie up soil nitrogen
and cause deficiencies in plants."*

I routinely use, and recommend, arborist wood chips as a land-scape mulch. Just as routinely, I am questioned about the nutrient deficiencies that wood-chip mulches will create in the soil. These woody mulches have a high carbon-to-nitrogen ratio, and microbes must scavenge other pockets of soil nitrogen during the decomposition process, allegedly making it unavailable to plants. Furthermore, woody materials that are used as amendments in soil or potting mixes will create zones of nitrogen deficiency, which is evidenced by the spindly, chlorotic growth of plants in these zones. Why, then, do I continue to recommend wood-chip mulches if they create nutrient problems for plants?

The Reality

Actually, arborist wood chips used as mulch neither bind up nitrogen nor inhibit the growth of established landscape plants. Woody mulches are slow to decompose, as they contain high levels of lignin and other biochemicals that resist microbial action. They are the ultimate "slow-release" fertilizer. Much of the microbial action takes place at the interface between the mulch and the soil; it is in this region that a nitrogen deficiency could occur. The roots of trees and shrubs, however, are primarily located below this interface.

I studied the relationship between wood chips and nitrogen deficiency in a replicated research experiment. What I found was that nitrogen levels at the mulch/soil interface were very low—definitely not enough for most plants. Yet less than one inch below the interface, the nitrogen levels were normal. These findings support two practical conclusions:

☙ Wood-chip mulches will not reduce the amount of nitrogen available to existing plants, whose roots are primarily below the mulch/soil interface.

☙ Wood-chip mulches will reduce the amount of nitrogen available to germinating seeds or seedlings, whose roots are primarily near the mulch/soil interface.

This first conclusion is validated by many studies demonstrating that woody mulches increase nutrient levels in both soils and plant foliage. In addition to serving as nutrient reservoirs, coarse woody mulches also conserve water, moderate temperature, and prevent the erosion and compaction of soils. Compared to the various other mulches studied, wood chips are superior choices in terms of the improved establishment and survival of urban trees and shrubs.

The second conclusion has been supported through several studies that find wood-chip mulches to be superior for weed control, compared to a variety of other materials. It's likely that microbial competition with weed seeds and seedlings for nitrogen is at least partially responsible for this phenomenon. For this reason, it is inadvisable to use wood chips or other low-nitrogen mulches in annual beds or vegetable gardens where desirable plants do not have deep root systems—and you definitely do not want to work them into the soil!

The lack of nitrogen in wood-chip mulches also discourages a number of insect pests, who generally prefer mulches with higher nitrogen and phosphorus content. Studies on subterranean termite (*Reticulitermes virginicus*) activity underneath both organic (bark and wood) and inorganic (gravel) mulches revealed that the greatest activity was found beneath the gravel mulch—an inedible material. Not only were the wood and bark mulches unappealing to termites, but when the insects were fed a diet of these materials in the lab, they suffered increased mortality.

If you are still concerned about nitrogen availability and wood-chips mulches, you can always create a thin layer of a more nutrient-rich mulch (like compost) underneath your wood chips. This "mulch sandwich" mimics what you would see in the mulch layer of a forest ecosystem. It's not required, though, as over time a wood-chip mulch will develop this same structure as the lower layers break down.

The Bottom Line

∿ Wood chips do not deplete soil nitrogen when they are used as a mulch.

∿ Wood-chip mulches are not attractive to termites.

∿ Wood-chip mulches create a soil environment that enhances plant establishment and growth.

∿ Wood-chip mulches decrease weed seed germination and survival.

References

Arthur, M. A., and Y. Wang. 1999. "Soil nutrients and microbial biomass following weed-control treatments in a Christmas tree plantation." *Soil Science Society of America Journal* 63:629–37.

Chalker-Scott, L. 2007. "Arborist wood chip mulches—Landscape boon or bane?" *MasterGardener* 1(3): 21–23.

Chalker-Scott, L. 2007. "Impact of mulches on landscape plants and the environment—A review." *Journal of Environmental Horticulture* 25(4): 239–49.

Duryea, M. L., J. B. Huffman, R. J. English, and W. Osbrink. 1999. "Will subterranean termites consume landscape mulches?" *Journal of Arboriculture* 25:143–49.

Greenly, K., and D. Rakow. 1995. "The effects of mulch type and depth on weed and tree growth." *Journal of Arboriculture* 21:225–32.

Long, C. E., B. L. Thorne, N. L. Breisch, and L. W. Douglass. 2001. "Effect of organic and inorganic landscape mulches on subterranean termite (Isoptera: Rhinotermitidae) foraging activity." *Environmental Entomology* 30:832–36.

Pickering, J. S., and A. Shepherd. 2000. "Evaluation of organic landscape mulches: Composition and nutrient release characteristics." *Arboricultural Journal* 23:175–87.

Szwedo, J., and M. Maszczyk. 2000. "Effects of straw-mulching of tree rows on some soil characteristics, mineral nutrient uptake and cropping of sour cherry trees." *Journal of Fruit and Ornamental Plant Research* 8:147–53.

Original article posted in July 2007.

THE MYTH OF
PATHOGENIC WOOD CHIPS

The Myth

*"Wood chips made from diseased trees will
spread pathogenic fungi and bacteria."*

Arborist wood chips as landscape mulches are increasing in popularity for several reasons: they tend to be cheap or free, they represent the reuse of a local resource, and they are functionally
superior to most other mulch materials. However, people do
worry about the source of their chips. If they come from trees
felled by a windstorm, that's fine—but what about if they come
from a diseased tree? Won't they infect the healthy roots of the
trees and shrubs in the landscape to which they are applied?

The Reality

Mulches made from diseased plant materials can contain pathogens; for this reason, many people compost their wood chips before using them. However, there is little scientific evidence that fresh wood chips are capable of transferring disease. Researchers have investigated the infectivity of wood chips containing common pathogens responsible for butt rot (*Armillaria gallica*), canker (*Botryosphaeria ribis*), shoestring rot (*Armillaria mellea*), and verticillium wilt (*Verticillium* spp.). In all cases, these deliberately infected mulches failed to transmit disease to healthy trees. The only documented evidence of disease transmission thus far occurred in Austrian pines (*Pinus nigra*) infected with tip blight (*Sphaeropsis sapinea*). When this material was used as a mulch around the healthy saplings of various tree species, only *P. nigra* saplings were infected (it should be noted that the researcher acknowledges that Austrian pine is particularly susceptible to tip blight). In other long-term studies, fresh wood chips have been used as mulch without any report of disease transmission.

It is not surprising that so few examples of mulched-mediated disease transmission have been documented. The pathogen of interest must be present in such a way as to fit the epidemiology of the disease cycle; simply existing in a mulch source is not enough. Under healthy soil conditions, beneficial and harmless fungi can outcompete pathogens for space on plant roots. Furthermore, healthy plants are not susceptible to opportunistic pathogens such as *Armillaria* and *Phytophthora*, which are often ubiquitous but inactive in well-managed soils. When soils become compacted and anaerobic, soil and plant health declines, and roots become susceptible to opportunistic pathogenic microbes.

Though the likelihood of mulch-mediated disease transmission to healthy plant roots is remote, it is important to keep

wood-chip mulches away from the trunks of trees and shrubs—
dark, moist conditions around trunk bark can enable pathogen
infection. And under no circumstances should wood mulch be
used as backfill! Not only is this a poor installation practice, but a
potential mechanism for disease transfer as well. A researcher
working with rhododendrons (*Rhododendron* spp.) lost plant
material to *Phytophthora* root rot after amending the soil with 33
percent composted wood chips. A similar transmittal of verticillium wilt (*Verticillium dahliae*) was seen when infected wood chips
were used as part of a potting mix. (Note that these findings also
cast doubt on the efficacy of composting to eliminate pathogens.)

The Bottom Line

- Wood-chip mulch made from diseased wood is unlikely to
  transmit disease to healthy roots.

- Healthy soils contain beneficial microbes that are antagonis-
  tic to many pathogens.

- If disease transmission is a concern, allow chips to age
  before using.

- Be sure to keep wood-chip mulches away from the trunks of
  trees and shrubs, as the bark could become vulnerable to
  pathogen infection.

- Do not incorporate wood chips as a soil amendment; in addition to causing nitrogen deficiency, they can spread disease
  to nearby roots.

๛ Keep soils well-aerated to prevent dormant pathogens in the soil from becoming infective.

References

Chalker-Scott, L. 2007. "Arborist wood chip mulches—Landscape boon or bane?" *MasterGardener* 1(3): 21–23.

Chalker-Scott, L. 2007. "Impact of mulches on landscape plants and the environment—A review." *Journal of Environmental Horticulture* 25(4): 239–49.

Foreman, G. L., D. I. Rouse, and B. D. Hudelson. 2002. "Wood chip mulch as a source of *Verticillium dahliae.*" *Phytopathology* 92:S26.

Hoover-Litty, H., and R. T. Hanlin. 1985. "The mycoflora of wood chips to be used as mulch." *Mycologia* 77(5): 721–31.

Jacobs, K. A. 2005. "The potential of mulch to transmit three tree pathogens." *Journal of Arboriculture* 31:235–41.

Koski, R., and W. R. Jacobi. 2004. "Tree pathogen survival in chipped wood mulch." *Journal of Arboriculture* 30:165–71.

Pair, J. C. 1994. "Adaptability of evergreen rhododendrons to the great plains as influenced by landscape exposure." *American Rhododendron Society Journal* 48:69–72.

Zauza, E. A. V., A. C. Alfenas, L. A. Maffia, S. F. da Silveira, and D. Fernandes. 2001. "Influence of mulch on the inoculum fluctuation of *Rhizoctonia* and *Cylindrocladium* on shoots and cuttings of *Eucalyptus grandis.*" *Summa Phytopathologica* 27(2): 213–17.

Original article posted in December 2002.

THE MYTH OF
RUBBERIZED LANDSCAPES

The Myth

*"Recycled rubber mulch is an environmentally
friendly, nontoxic choice for landscapes."*

Discarded rubber tires are the bane of waste management.
According to the EPA, we generate 290 million scrap tires annually. Scrap tire stockpiles can pose significant fire hazards; the
1983 Virginia tire fire burned for nine months when one such
stockpile caught fire. Obviously, finding a market for these slow-to-decompose materials is desirable, and many innovative uses
have been developed, including rubberized playground surfaces,
asphalt, and landscape mulches. From an engineering standpoint, crumb rubber as a soil amendment has performed favorably in reducing compaction to specialty landscape surfaces such
as sports fields and putting greens.

Rubber mulches are touted by manufacturers and distributors as permanent ("doesn't decay away") and aesthetically pleasing ("no odor"—"looks like shredded wood mulch"—"earth tones and designer colors"—"special fade resistant coating") landscape materials. Furthermore, we are told that rubber mulch is "safe for flowers, plants and pets" (though it "doesn't feed or house insects") and "dramatically improves landscaping." It seems to be an environmentally friendly solution to a major waste-disposal problem.

The Reality

Rubber mulches have not proved to be particularly good choices for either horticultural production or landscape uses. In comparison studies of several mulch types, rubber-tire mulch was less effective in controlling weeds in herbaceous perennial plots than were wood chips. Similarly, sawdust made a better mulch for Christmas tree production in terms of weed control, microbial biomass, and soil chemistry. Another comparative study found rubber to be less effective than straw or fiber mulch in establishing turfgrasses.

Not only do rubber mulches perform less effectively in the landscape, they possess an additional, unwanted characteristic. Compared to a dozen other mulch types, ground rubber is more likely to ignite and more difficult to extinguish. In areas where the possibility of natural or man-made fires is significant, rubber mulches should not be used.

Rubber mulches are touted as permanent groundcover for landscapes. But far from being permanent, rubber is broken down by microbes like any other organic product. Many bacterial species have been isolated and identified that are capable of utilizing rubber as their sole energy source. Such bacteria have been found in a variety of environments, including the cavity water of discarded tires. Although some of the additives used in tire manufacture are toxic to rubber-degrading bacteria, there are white-rot and brown-rot fungal species that can detoxify these additives. While isolating these microbes has been beneficial in developing natural mechanisms to recycle rubber products, it also points out the fallacy of assuming that rubber mulch is "permanent." Furthermore, it alerts us to the very real possibility that car tires leach toxic compounds into the landscape.

Rubber mulches are reassuringly advertised as being nontoxic to people, pets, and the environment. However, current research at Bucknell University indicates that rubber leachate from car tires can kill entire aquatic communities of algae, zooplankton, snails, and fish. At lower concentrations, the leachates cause reproductive problems and precancerous lesions. A similar study exploring the use of tires as artificial reef substrates also found rubber leachate to negatively affect the survival of various seaweeds and phytoplankton. Marine and other saline environments are less sensitive to tire leachates, however, and the greatest threat of contamination appears to be to freshwater habitats.

Part of the toxic nature of rubber leachate is due to its metal content: aluminum, cadmium, chromium, copper, iron, magnesium, manganese, molybdenum, selenium, sulfur, and zinc have all been identified in laboratory and field leachates. If rubber products have been exposed to contaminants, such as lead or other heavy metals, during their useful lifetime, they will adsorb these metals and release them as well. Of these metals, rubber contains very high levels of zinc—as much as 2 percent of the tire mass. A number of plant species, including landscape materials, have been shown to accumulate abnormally high levels of zinc—sometimes to the point of death. One USDA researcher who for decades has studied zinc and other metals in soils and plant materials strongly believes that ground rubber should not be used "in any composting, or in any potting medium, or casually dispersed on agricultural or garden soils" because of zinc toxicity. Acidic soils are particularly sensitive, since heavy metals are more easily released under acidic conditions and become available to plant and animal uptake.

Rubber leachates are complex solutions. They include not only the minerals and organic building blocks of rubber but also various plasticizers and accelerators used during the vulcanizing process. In high enough concentrations, some of these rubber leachates are known to be harmful to human health; effects of exposure range from skin and eye irritation to major organ damage and even death. Long-term exposure can lead to neurological damage, carcinogenesis, and mutagenesis.

Some of these materials break down quickly, while others are known to accumulate through the food web. One of the more common rubber leachates is 2-mercaptobenzothiazole, a common accelerator for rubber vulcanization. In addition to its possible carcinogenic effects on humans, it is highly persistent in the environment and very toxic to aquatic organisms; its environmental persistence may cause long-term damage to aquatic environments constantly exposed to rubber leachates. Other organic leachates under scrutiny are the polyaromatic hydrocarbons (PAHs). These compounds, used as rubber softeners and fillers, have been repeatedly demonstrated to be toxic to aquatic life. PAHs are released continually into solution, and after two years in a laboratory test, leachates were shown to be even more toxic than at the study's inception.

It is abundantly clear from the scientific literature that rubber should not be used as a landscape amendment or mulch. There is no doubt that toxic substances leach from rubber as it degrades, contaminating the soil, landscape plants, and associated aquatic systems. While recycling waste tires is an important issue to address, it is not a solution to simply move the problem to our landscapes and surface waters.

The Bottom Line

~ Rubber mulch is not as effective as other organic mulch choices in controlling weeds.

~ Rubber mulch is highly flammable and difficult to extinguish once it is burning.

~ Rubber mulch is not permanent; like other organic substances, it decomposes.

~ Rubber mulch is not nontoxic; it contains a number of metal and organic contaminants with known environmental and/ or human health effects.

References

Azizian, M. F., P. O. Nelson, P. Thayumanavan, and K. J. Williamson. 2001. "Environmental impact of crumb rubber asphalt concrete leachate contaminants from highway construction and repair materials on surface and ground waters." *American Chemical Society Abstracts* 221(1–2): ENVR 15.

Bush, E., K. Leader, and A. Owings. 2001. "Foliar accumulation of zinc in tree species grown in pine bark media amended with crumb rubber." *Journal of Plant Nutrition* 24(3): 503–10.

Chalker-Scott, L. 2007. "Impact of mulches on landscape plants and the environment—A review." *Journal of Environmental Horticulture* 25(4): 239–49.

Christiansson, M., B. Stenberg, and O. Holst. 2000. "Toxic additives: A problem for microbial waste rubber desulphurization." *Resource and Environmental Biotechnology* 3(1): 11–21.

Gualtieri, M., M. Milani, M. Camatini, M. Andrioletti, and C. Vismara. 2005. "Toxicity of tire debris leachates." *Environment International* 31(5): 723–30.

Mirfendereski, G. "Crumb Rubber." SynTurf. http://www.synturf.org/crumbrubber.html. Accessed February 2, 2009.

San-Miguel, G., G. D. Fowler, and C. J. Sollars. 2002. "The leaching of inorganic species from activated carbons produced from waste tyre rubber." *Water Research* 36(8): 1939–46.

Smolders, E., and F. Degryse. 2002. "Fate and effect of zinc from tire debris in soil." *Environmental Science and Technology* 36(17): 3706–10.

Stephensen, E., M. Adolfsson-Erici, M. Celander, M. Hulander, J. Parkkonen, T. Hegelund, J. Sturve, L. Hasselberg, M. Bengtsson, and L. Forlin. 2003. "Biomarker responses and chemical analyses in fish indicate leakage of polycyclic aromatic hydrocarbons and other compounds from car tire rubber." *Environmental Toxicology and Chemistry* 22(12): 2926–31.

Steward, L. G., T. D Sydnor, and B. Bishop. 2003. "The ease of ignition of 13 landscape mulches." *Journal of Arboriculture* 29(6): 317–21.

Wik, A., and G. Dave. 2005. "Environmental labeling of car tires—Toxicity to *Daphnia magna* can be used as a screening method." *Chemosphere* 58(5): 645–51.

Original article posted in September 2005.

THE MYTH OF
PHYTOTOXIC YARD WASTE

The Myth

"Uncomposted yard waste mulch is harmful to
plant life and negatively impacts water quality."

A few years ago I received a draft of a document addressing a "local problem": "utilizing ground green waste as mulch." In short, this document states that yard waste (defined as woody and green materials) is being used improperly as a mulch for streambed restoration, erosion control, and weed and moisture control. The argument that this material "is likely causing harm to plant life and may be negatively impacting water quality and plant life" is followed by a bulleted list of specific problems attributed to use of immature composts. These include (1) oxygen reduction in the root zone; (2) nitrogen depletion of the soil;

(3) "altering stable forms of nitrogen existing in the soil into mobile forms tending to runoff with moisture"; (4) introduction of plant disease; (5) introduction of phytotoxic compounds; (6) introduction of weed seeds; (7) introduction of pesticides; (8) contamination of surface waters by "organic acids, phenolic compounds, ammonia and ethylene"; and (9) "release of oxygen depleted water" into surface waters. The document ends by stating, "There are beneficial uses of mulch if the mulch is made from the proper materials, mainly woody debris devoid of nitrogen sources such as leaves, needles or grasses. To gain most of the attributes of mulch along with providing a nutrient source, greater moisture retention, biofiltration and disease suppression then cured compost should be utilized."

The Reality

In *The Informed Gardener*, I documented the benefits that arborist wood chips and other coarse organic mulches can offer to a landscape. Rather than repeat those here, let's address each of the problems outlined above and sort out fact from fiction.

First of all, we need to clarify the difference between yard waste and immature compost. There are a number of published studies that document the problems with using immature composts, many of which are listed above. However, these studies are focused on immature composts made from biosolids, municipal solid waste, manures, and other high-nitrogen materials—not yard wastes. Yard wastes, even with significant amounts of green material, are not particularly rich in nitrogen; in fact, they can cause nitrogen deficiencies if amended into the soil rather than used as a mulch. This distinction allows us to exempt yard-waste mulch from many of the hazards of immature composts—specifically, any type of runoff or toxicity associated with nitrogen (points 3 and 8). Likewise, the phytotoxic compounds referred to in points 5 and 8—including salts, fatty acids, etc.—are associated with immature composts made from biosolids and municipal solid wastes, not plant materials (it should be noted that ethylene is a gas and would not be a water contaminant). There is no evidence that decomposing yard wastes generate any quantity of these substances or contribute to surface water contamination. Indeed, the presence of coarse mulch material will help reduce water runoff and increase the immobilization of potentially harmful materials.

Point 2—nitrogen deficiency of the soil—will be a problem if yard wastes are incorporated into the soil. However, numerous observations and anecdotal evidence suggest that no such deficiency occurs when yard wastes are used as a mulch. As discussed in a previous chapter, a zone of nitrogen deficiency exists at the mulch/soil interface, inhibiting seed germination (weed control!), while having no effect on established plant roots below the surface.

Next let's consider the issue of oxygen depletion. With a coarse mulch, even applied to a depth of several inches, there is no zone of oxygen depletion. Water and gases move easily through the mulch to the soil, and in fact can improve this movement by protecting the soil surface from compaction. Points 1 and 9 are therefore eliminated from consideration.

The issue of contaminated mulch has also been discussed in a previous chapter, so I will briefly summarize the problem. Plant material treated with pesticides should not be used as mulch, nor should weeds with seed heads be added to the mix. This is an invitation to trouble. But I must mention that even mature composts are subject to contamination, especially by persistent pesticides (clopyralid-contaminated compost was a significant problem a few years ago). Therefore, points 6 and 7 can be easily avoided in yard waste mulch but may be harder to avoid in commercially available compost, whose origins are harder to identify.

Point 4 is the only possible area of concern and, again, was addressed in an earlier chapter. There is little evidence linking the transmission of disease from mulch material to living plants in a landscape. Although we know that healthy soils increase plant health and reduce susceptibility to disease, and although it appears that the use of mulch will promote these benefits, it is probably best to avoid using heavily diseased materials as mulch.

Finally, all one has to do to see what has worked as a mulch for eons is to visit any natural ecosystem: dead plant material settles on the soil surface without any prior composting, and the landscape does just fine.

The Bottom Line

~ Uncomposted, clean yard waste is a natural mulch with demonstrated benefits to landscape plantings and soil health.

~ If plant material has been treated with pesticides or contains weed seeds, it should not be used as mulch.

~ Yard waste mulch may be a poor choice for use in annual flower beds and vegetable gardens where seedlings, rather than established plants, are present.

References

Bahe, A. R., and C. H. Peacock. 1995. "Bioavailable herbicide residues in turfgrass clippings used for mulch adversely affect plant growth." *HortScience* 30(7): 1393–95.

Casale, W. L., V. Minassian, J. A. Menge, C. J. Lovatt, E. Pond, E. Johnson, and F. Guillemet. 1995. "Urban and agricultural wastes for use as mulches on avocado and citrus and for delivery of microbial biocontrol agents." *Journal of Horticultural Science* 70(2): 315–32.

Chalker-Scott, L. 2007. "Impact of mulches on landscape plants and the environment—A review." *Journal of Environmental Horticulture* 25(4): 239–49.

Daugovish, O., J. Downer, B. Faber, and M. McGiffen. 2007. "Weed survival in yard waste mulch." *Weed Technology* 21(1): 59–65.

de Costa, J. L. S, J. A. Menge, and W. L. Casale. 1996. "Investigations on some of the mechanisms by which bioenhanced mulches can suppress *Phytophthora* root rot of avocado." *Microbiological Research* 151(2): 183–92.

Ettlin, L., and B. Stewart. 1993. "Yard debris compost for erosion control." *Biocycle* 34(12): 46–47.

Foshee, W. G., W. D. Goff, K. M. Tilt, J. D. Williams, J. S. Bannon, and J. B. Witt. 1996. "Organic mulches increase growth of young pecan trees." *HortScience* 31(5): 811–12.

Harrell, M. S., and G. L. Miller. 2005. "Composted yard waste affects soil displacement and roadside vegetation." *HortScience* 40(7): 2157–63.

Persyn, R. A., T. D. Glanville, T. L. Richard, J. M. Laflen, and P. M. Dixon. 2004. "Environmental effects of applying composted organics to new highway embankments: Part 1. Interrill runoff and erosion." *Transactions of the ASAE* 47(2): 463–69.

Original article posted in May 2003.

WHY BUYING LADYBUGS
FOR YOUR GARDEN IS A BAD IDEA

While many gardeners believe that the planned release of beneficial insects is a recent development in managing pests, in fact this practice was established long ago. As early as 1924, ladybugs (more accurately called "lady beetles") were collected from the Sierra Nevada for release in California's Imperial Valley to control aphids on crops. Widely distributed throughout North America, this lady beetle is a voracious consumer of aphids and other insects. But recently researchers have raised concerns over the unintended ecological consequences of using nonindigenous insects for biological control:

- Harvesting and distributing California lady beetles can unwittingly spread their parasites and diseases over the entire country. Not only will this undermine the success of the imported lady beetles, but these natural enemies can attack local lady beetle species.

- Native lady beetles and other beneficial insects are endangered when new competitors are introduced to their ecosystem. For instance, the multicolored Asian lady beetle is able to tolerate a wide range of environmental conditions and pathogens, to reproduce and mature rapidly, to hunt and consume prey efficiently, to eat pollen and other plant foods when insect prey are scarce, and to consume the eggs and larvae of the local insect competitors. This and other nonindigenous lady beetles compete with and reduce populations of native predators, including lady beetles.

- Finally, the success of lady beetle capture-and-release programs is questionable. Early researchers reported that lady beetles captured in the Sierra Nevada and released at lower elevations immediately flew away. The most successful releases tend to be in nursery settings with high numbers of aphid-infested plants; open releases to gardens or landscape settings are generally not successful.

While the benefits of intentionally releasing some beneficial insects, such as lacewings, may outweigh the costs, the same cannot be said for lady beetles. Instead, it's best to create gardens and landscapes that attract and support indigenous beneficial insects.

MIRACLES IN A
BAG/BOTTLE/BOX

THE MYTH OF ANTITRANSPIRANTS

The Myth

"Antitranspirants prevent drought stress,
especially in newly installed trees and shrubs."

"Product X dries on plants to form a clear, glossy film that reduces water loss on plants while at the same time allowing them to breathe normally. Product X beautifies plants by polishing leaf surfaces."

"Product Y locks moisture and protects against winter kill, wind burn, and drought."

"Product Z is an antitranspirant and surfactant, which has been proved to minimise the impact of drought. Product Z is a balanced combination of amino acids, peptides and low molecular weight oligopeptides impregnated in a herbal based fatty alcohol series along with surfactants and biostimulant. Product Z imparts drought tolerance by reducing the rate of transpiration by regulating stomatal movements and increasing the rate of photosynthesis and carbohydrate reserves in roots. Proteins and peptides are complex structures playing a fundamental role in plant physiology. They function as growth activators in enzymatic systems and accelerate all the metabolic processes in the nutrient transformation."

Here are three examples of products that promise to reduce water use and increase survival of landscape plants. (We're going to ignore the ludicrous claim that amino acids applied to leaves do anything but feed bacteria.) Antitranspirants are recommended for preventing drought conditions in plants induced by wind, high temperatures, or cold temperatures. They are extolled as effective disease controllers and aids to plant propagation. They are used to preserve cut flowers and Christmas trees. What's not to like?

The Reality

Antitranspirant products can act as either physical or physiological barriers to leaf water loss (over 90 percent of the water in an actively growing plant is lost through the leaves). The most popularly used antitranspirants are spray emulsions of latex, wax, or acrylic that form a film over the leaf surface and reduce water loss. Solar reflectant products are also physical barriers that reduce internal leaf temperature and thereby depress evapotranspiration (the process by which water normally moves through a plant;

evaporation from the leaves helps pull water up from the roots). Antitranspirant products that form physiological barriers are those with chemicals that may close stomates or inhibit plant growth. Applying any of these antitranspirant products to plant leaves can have a significant impact on normal physiological function. Film-forming antitranspirants prevent evapotranspiration by covering and clogging leaf stomates—the tiny pores on leaf surfaces. These pores have two functions: they create a gradient for water movement throughout the plant and they allow gas exchange between the plant and the atmosphere. Each of these physiological functions is vital to a plant's survival. The transpiration stream not only moves water through the plant but transports root-produced growth regulators and soil minerals as well. Furthermore, water transpiration from the leaf surface aids in evaporative cooling of leaves. Interfering with this normal and necessary process is harmful to the plant; the increase in internal leaf temperature has been documented to kill some plants.

The second vital function performed by stomates is gas exchange. In the daytime, carbon dioxide enters the leaf and oxygen exits; in the evening, the reverse occurs. This is erroneously referred to as "breathing," but the metaphor is useful. Without carbon dioxide uptake, the photosynthetic rate is depressed. Regardless of what advertisers claim, it is impossible to prevent water vapor movement through the stomates without impairing gas exchange.

The scientific literature on antitranspirants is robust; numerous antitranspirants have been tested for their effect upon desiccation, disease control, fruit production, transplant establishment, and weed control. Controlled research has been conducted in the lab, greenhouse, nursery, and field on a variety of plants, ranging from vegetable crops to house plants to fruit and timber species.

Briefly, this is what recent research in the peer-reviewed literature has shown:

- DISEASE CONTROL. Antitranspirants decreased or did not affect bacterial and fungal diseases.

- FRUIT PRODUCTION. Antitranspirants increased, decreased, or did not affect fruit splitting; decreased or did not affect marketable yield; increased water loss from fruit.

- HEAT- OR COLD-INDUCED DESICCATION. Antitranspirants had no effect.

- ROOT/TUBER PRODUCTION. Antitranspirants delayed or had no effect on the growth of cuttings, though one study showed improved accumulation of calcium in roots and tubers.

- TRANSPLANT STRESS. Antitranspirants increased, decreased, or had no effect on survival; increased, decreased, or had no effect on transpiration; increased, decreased, or had no effect on leaf water content; reduced growth rate; decreased height; increased or decreased fresh and dry weight; delayed leaf unfolding; increased leaf drop; had no effect on root regeneration; decreased evaporative cooling and increased leaf temperature; depressed chlorophyll content.

- WEED CONTROL. Antitranspirants decreased transpiration, increased leaf temperature, and thereby increased weed mortality.

Plants vary significantly in their abilities to control leaf water loss: cuticle thickness, leaf pubescence, cell wall thickness, stomatal conductance, stomatal density, stomatal location (upper, lower, or both leaf surfaces), and leaf angle are species-specific characteristics that affect rates of water loss. Furthermore, environmental conditions vary significantly between controlled laboratory settings, greenhouses, and field research situations. It's not surprising that research results are contradictory.

For millions of years, plants have survived the so-called "photosynthesis-transpiration compromise," which describes the simultaneous uptake of carbon dioxide and loss of water through the leaf stomates. Each species is adapted to the environmental conditions under which it evolved. If a plant suffers from extreme drought stress, it's likely that site conditions aren't optimal for that species. Interfering with the plant's ability to manufacture food by blocking stomates is only going to increase the stress load, which could be lethal to plants already shocked from transplanting or other environmental perturbations.

The Bottom Line

๛ While applied antitranspirants prevent stomatal water loss, they also increase heat load, inhibit gas exchange, and decrease photosynthesis.

๛ Use of antitranspirants is not recommended for gardens and landscapes; instead, follow gardening practices that both reduce water usage and drought stress.

๛ Choose site-appropriate plants; know the water needs of selected species and plant accordingly.

∞ Species with large, thin leaves are more sensitive to water stress than those with small, thick leaves or needles.

∞ A little water stress is a good thing; it will help acclimate the plant to future drought.

∞ There is no substitute for adequate soil water conditions.

∞ Maintain adequate soil moisture in newly installed land-scapes through mulching and other sustainable practices.

∞ Maintain optimal soil temperatures through mulching; cooler soils have less evaporation.

References

Brooks, K. N., and D. B. Thorud. 1971. "Antitranspirant effects on the transpiration and physiology of *Tamarisk.*" *Water Resources Research* 7(3): 499–51.

Chaney, W. R., and T. T. Kozlowski. 1973. "Growth and transpiration of black locust seedlings in soil with incorporated cetyl alcohol." *Canadian Journal of Forest Research* 3(4): 604–6.

Clement, D. L., S. A. Gill, and W. Potts. 1994. "Alternatives for powdery mildew control on lilac." *Journal of Arboriculture* 20(4): 227–30.

Gottwald, T. R., and J. H. Graham. 1997. "The influence of spray adjuvants on exacerbation of citrus bacterial spot." *Plant Disease* 81(11): 1305–10.

Hummel, R. L. 1990. "Water relations of container-grown woody and herbaceous plants following antitranspirant sprays." *HortScience* 25(7): 772–75.

Koffmann, W., N. L. Wade, and H. Nicol. 1996. "Tree sprays and root pruning fail to control rain induced cracking of sweet cherries." *Plant Protection Quarterly* 11(3): 126–30.

Press, M. C., J. J. Nour, F. F. Bebawi, and G. R. Stewart. 1989. "Antitranspirant-induced heat stress in the parasitic plant *Striga hermonthica*—A novel method of control." *Journal of Experimental Botany* 40(214): 585–91.

Ranney, T. G., N. L. Bassuk, and T. H. Whitlow. 1989. "Effect of transplanting practices on growth and water relations of 'Colt' cherry trees during reestablishment." *Journal of Environmental Horticulture* 7(1): 41–45.

Wang, Y. T., K. H. Hsiao, and L. L. Gregg. 1992. "Antitranspirant, water stress, and growth retardant influence growth of golden pothos." *HortScience* 27(3): 222–25.

Warmund, M. R., C. E. Finn, and C. J. Starbuck. 1995. "Yield of micropropagated 'Allen' black raspberry plants reduced by bark mulch, shade cloth and Folicote." *Journal of Small Fruit and Viticulture* 3(1): 15–24.

Original article posted in September 2002.

THE MYTH OF
BUBBLY COMPOST TEA

The Myth

"Aerobically brewed compost tea suppresses disease."

No "Myth" topic has generated more interest, or controversy, than the purported ability of compost teas to suppress disease (a topic I introduced in *The Informed Gardener*). With few exceptions, popular and industry magazines extol the virtues of aerated compost teas (ACTs)—what I refer to in the above title as "bubbly tea." Literature for the gardening public uses phrases such as "lush foliage," "beautiful blooms," "delicious fruits and vegetables," and "thick green turf" to describe the effect of compost tea on particular plants. More broadly, usage of ACT is promised to "improve all soils," "provide beneficial organisms," and "keep garden plants, turf, and crops free of disease." Environmental benefits are guaranteed, too: it is claimed that ACT "reduces dependence on chemicals" and "reduces fertilizer use and leaching into ground water." An industry article reports that "several studies have successfully controlled plant diseases and increased plant growth with compost teas," though no evidence was presented to support this claim.

Since I first investigated compost tea claims in 2001, Google hits on .com sites alone increased from 1,900 at that time to over 80,000 eight years later. An article in the trade magazine *Biocycle* states that the compost tea industry is growing at an estimated 25 percent per year. Obviously, with events of recent years, the marketing of compost tea for disease suppression has become a bigger business. Has the science behind the practice grown as well?

The Reality

Two recent literature reviews on the role of compost tea in disease control report that non-aerated compost tea (NCT) can be effective in reducing some foliar pathogens in laboratory, greenhouse, and field studies (Litterick et al. 2004, and Scheuerell and Mahaffee 2002). NCTs are passively made by running water through compost, require no special equipment, and cost virtually nothing to produce. In contrast, there are very few published studies on ACT efficacy. This doesn't mean that ACTs aren't being researched, however. In addition to the articles cited in the two review papers, the Internet contains a number of research reports from university scientists recently or currently involved in ACT research. A number of different bacterial and fungal diseases have been studied, including mildews, rots, spots, and wilts, on a variety of different crops, including fruits, vegetables, roses, and turf grasses. One study—on greenhouse-grown grapes—found some success in controlling both botrytis and powdery mildew. The remaining studies—all conducted in the field—found ACTs to be ineffective.

This represents the current state of university science behind the efficacy of aerated compost tea in disease control. Will these results be published in the peer-reviewed scientific literature? One hopes so, but the reality is that many scientists don't publish "negative" results and instead move on to other, more promising areas of research. This is unfortunate, as the science behind compost tea is very young and requires, as all researchers agree, substantial research before the hypothesis of disease control can be supported.

What do compost tea producers say about these negative results? Often they criticize the tea microbial content, the tea brewing process, the application process, weather conditions, other environmental stresses, etc.—in other words, they assert that the fault is not with the product. However, the overwhelming lack of positive results in university ACT studies suggests that the hypothesis—that ACTs suppress plant diseases—might be in error and need to be revised. Even if the criticisms of the research results are justified, how realistic can such a technology be for typical home owners who want to make and apply their own compost tea?

The real problem I see in the world of compost tea is the selling of a product whose efficacy is based on faith rather than science. As one proponent states, "There is no doubt in my mind that compost tea has already proven to be beneficial to agriculture." Individuals with this mind-set are not open to having their beliefs challenged by scientists or anyone else. However, buying expensive "tea brewers," purchasing ready-made "tea" at several dollars a gallon, or paying a company to apply ACT in the absence of objective data sounds like snake oil sales rather than science.

There are thousands of Web sites with glowing anecdotal praise for compost tea used as a foliar spray. What seems to be missing are stories from the other side—from those business and homeowners who haven't seen differences in disease control or have even noted increased incidence and severity of disease. There is no scientific evidence for ACT disease control on turf or landscape materials. Since ACT is not registered by the EPA as a pesticide, it is illegal to recommend its use as one, or to apply it as such to another person's landscape. Though some commercial sites disclose this regulatory fact, they also coyly include anecdotal information extolling the disease-suppressing properties of their product. Laundering product information to get around federal pesticide regulations is unethical. Misrepresentation of the science behind compost tea represents, at best, decisions based on faith rather than science. At worst, it suggests corporate profits at the expense of well-meaning but gullible consumers.

A final concern regarding compost tea is the discovery of human pathogens, such as *Escherichia coli*, in some ACTs. Though discussion of the topic is beyond the scope of this book, fecal contamination of compost teas continues to be a health issue of serious concern to the EPA and other agencies.

The Bottom Line

∾ Aerated compost tea (ACT) is not effective in treating plant disease in gardens or landscapes, and, since it is not registered as a pesticide, cannot legally be recommended or applied as one.

- ACTs have been demonstrated to harbor human pathogens, including *E. coli.*

- There is a rapidly growing compost tea industry that continues to downplay not only the lack of scientific evidence but also the documented health concerns behind its product.

- Garden and landscape products and practices should be based on objective plant and soil science, not on blind faith or commercial gain, as seems to be the case with ACTs.

References
(updates in addition to those in *The Informed Gardener*)

Chalker-Scott, L. 2008. "The Myth of Compost Tea." In *The Informed Gardener*, 169–74. University of Washington Press, Seattle, WA.

Chalker-Scott, L. 2008. "The Myth of Compost Tea Revisited." In *The Informed Gardener*, 175–80. University of Washington Press, Seattle, WA.

Daami-Remadi, M., H. Jabnoun-Khiareddine, F. Ayed, K. Hibar, I. E. A. Znaidi, and M. El-Mahjoub. 2006. "In vitro and in vivo evaluation of individually compost fungi for potato *Fusarium* dry rot biocontrol." *Journal of Biological Sciences* 6(3): 572–80.

Drenovsky, R. E., R. A. Duncan, and K. M. Scow. 2005. "Soil sterilization and organic carbon, but not microbial inoculants, change microbial communities in replanted peach orchards." *California Agriculture* 59(3): 176–81.

Gils, J., C. Chong, and G. Lumis. 2005. "Response of container-grown ninebark to crude and nutrient-enriched recirculating compost leachates." *Hortscience* 40(5): 1507–12.

Hall, S. G., D. A. Schellinger, and W. A. Carney. 2006. "Enhancing sugarcane field residue biodegradation by grinding and use of compost tea." *Compost Science and Utilization* 14(1): 32–39.

Jarecki, M. K., C. Chong, and R. P. Voroney. 2005. "Evaluation of compost leachates for plant growth in hydroponic culture." *Journal of Plant Nutrition* 28(4): 651–67.

Keeling, A. A., K. R. McCallum, and C. P. Beckwith. 2003. "Mature green waste compost enhances growth and nitrogen uptake in wheat (*Triticum aestivum* L.) and oilseed rape (*Brassica napus* L.) through the action of water-extractable factors." *Bioresource Technology* 90(2): 127–32.

Litterick, A. M., L. Harrier, P. Wallace, C. A. Watson, and M. Wood. 2004. "The role of uncomposted materials, composts, manures, and compost extracts in reducing pest and disease incidence and severity in sustainable temperate a gricultural and horticultural crop production—A review." *Critical Reviews in Plant Sciences* 23(6): 453–79.

Scheuerell, S., and W. Mahaffee. 2002. "Compost tea: Principles and prospects for plant disease control." *Compost Science and Utilization* 10(4): 313–38.

Original article posted in October 2005.

THE MYTH OF
CURATIVE KELP

The Myth

*"Seaweed extracts reduce disease, improve production,
and increase stress resistance in landscape plants."*

Seaweeds are ancient relatives of terrestrial plants and play a similar ecological role as the "forest" in coastal marine ecosystems. Collectively, kelps are the larger seaweed species and are also of historical dietary and medicinal importance to various human societies. Their extracts have extensive industrial applications, and, more recently, their activity as antioxidants and antibiotics has been investigated. It is clear that human consumption of some seaweeds imparts health benefits; can seaweeds also benefit plant health?

Vendors of natural garden products certainly want you to think so. Web sites and sales literature praise the effectiveness of seaweed extracts as soil conditioners, plant disease suppressants, and stress reducers. Unverified research is presented to support the use of seaweed drenches or sprays on turf, fruits and vegetables, flowers, perennials, shrubs, and trees in every imaginable situation. Are seaweed extracts that elusive magic bullet for creating perfect landscapes?

The Reality

Seaweed extracts (SE) have been dubbed "biostimulants" or "metabolic enhancers," defined as chemicals with growth-enhancing properties but little nutrient value. Growth enhancement has been attributed to the presence of plant growth regulators (sometimes called plant hormones), and several of these growth regulators have been isolated from seaweed extracts, including cytokinins, auxins, and gibberellins. This is not surprising, as seaweeds are part of the plant kingdom and, like other plants, manufacture their own growth regulators. More important is the question of whether these substances might have similar regulatory effects when applied to garden and landscape plants.

There is a substantial body of scientific literature on the application of seaweed extracts in agriculture, in some cases dating back nearly a century. Much of the earlier research suggested benefits from SE treatment, but more recent results have been cautious in recommending SE use. I've compiled a brief summary of these research findings:

1   ROOTING. Logic suggests that the growth regulators found in SE, like any other commercially available rooting hormone, can stimulate root development on cuttings and transplants. This suggestion is borne out in research on both potatoes and pines in laboratory and greenhouse applications, where SE could have use as a root dip during transplanting. Success would not be expected (nor has it been found) in field applications to existing plants, as these compounds are quickly degraded by microbes and are unlikely to have any regulatory effect on nearby plant tissues.

2   TURF HEALTH. There has been some success in utilizing seaweed extracts as a turf-enhancing treatment. Research has focused predominantly on Kentucky bluegrass, where SE applications have been associated with improved seedling establishment, rooting, and increased drought and salinity tolerance. However, other research with the same plant material reported "little effect" after SE treatment. Seaweed extracts are also reported to improve root growth of bentgrass and improve the "physical strength" of environmentally stressed turf.

3   FOLIAR GROWTH. Other than the aforementioned turf benefits, there are few, if any, documented advantages of SE application to plant foliage. Treatment of cabbage resulted in no change in either head yield or nutrient content; similarly, in apples neither vegetative growth nor leaf mineral content was altered.

4   FRUIT AND VEGETABLE SIZE, YIELD AND/OR QUALITY. Many studies have examined SE efficacy in

improving fruit and vegetable production. Some positive, albeit inconsistent, results have been found in apples, apricots, citrus, and peaches. More often, however, SE treatment does not improve production of tested crops, including bush and wax beans, cabbages, sweet corn, cucumbers, pears, peppers, persimmons, strawberries, or tomatoes.

5   DISEASE MANAGEMENT. There are few reports of successful disease management through SE application. Positive results were found in greenhouse-grown cabbage and carrots, where seaweed extract prevented disease. Other experiments on bacterial and fungal control have had less success. Grain treated with SE was no more resistant to subsequent fungal infection, but germination rates actually decreased as a result. SE treatment of strawberry fungal infection and bacterial leaf spot in tomato had only a 33 percent success rate, while investigations on *Alternaria* leaf blight and peach leaf curl showed no effect. Likewise, SE had no effect on treating fungal disease in potatoes.

6   PEST MANAGEMENT. A forty-year-old report suggested that seaweed extract would decrease red spider mite infestations. Nothing more has developed from that initial hypothesis, but a number of more recent papers have documented the nematicidal activity of some seaweed extracts. Researchers have found reduced egg production and hatching and increased larval mortality in nematodes treated directly with seaweed extract. Applied to greenhouse plants, seaweed extracts reduced nematode infestation of tomato plants and citrus species, but no effect was found on field-grown citrus. In contrast, SE-treated lima beans and tomatoes were

preferred by an insect pest, and had the unfortunate side
effect of inhibiting lima bean growth.

7   ENVIRONMENTAL STRESS RESISTANCE. Virtually no
success has been reported in this area; while the earlier-men-
tioned turf work suggested that SE application improved
salinity and drought tolerance, that effect does not carry over
to other plants, especially not landscape plant species. In
two separate studies, seaweed extract was unsuccessful in
improving plant growth or transplant survival of five common ornamental shrubs and trees (arborvitae, callery pear,
holly, oak, and spiraea). In fact, untreated plants mulched
with pine bark performed better than those that received a
commercial product containing "a blend of endo- and ecto-
mycorrhizal fungi, beneficial root/soil bacteria, chelated
micronutrients and biocatalysts including humic acids, complex carbohydrates, yucca plant extract, sea kelp and organic
N and P." In another study, compost was found to be more
effective in drought resistance than biostimulants including
seaweed extracts.

In terms of practical application, researchers have concluded
the following:

⌇ PLANT SELECTION. "Working with resistant varieties
seems to be the best solution [to disease resistance]."

⌇ ENVIRONMENTAL CONDITIONS. "Soil fertility and production conditions were more important growth and yield
determinants than were foliar sprays."

∾ MANAGEMENT TECHNIQUES. "If proper planting techniques are followed, the use of biostimulants is unwar-
ranted."

∾ OVERALL ASSESSMENT. "Treatments are ultimately
dependent on multiple plant, soil, and environmental factors, and often have no discernible effects." "There appears
to be little value in applying these products."

∾ MARKETING. "Manufacturers' claims for the benefits of
these products go beyond what is substantiated by the
research." "The number of products now on the market
seems to outnumber the published papers."

These researchers' conclusions say it all—seaweed extracts
are aggressively marketed, with little regard for objective, scientific research. There is a final concern never addressed, which is
the justification for large-scale removal of vegetation from one
ecosystem (marine kelp "forests") for application to another (terrestrial landscapes). The ecological impacts of increased seaweed
harvesting are currently under investigation and the possibility of
significant ecosystem damage is real. There is no argument that
seaweed products are useful and valuable to humans for the reasons discussed earlier. However, given that there are few documented benefits from applying seaweed extracts to plants, this is
neither a justifiable nor sustainable practice. The marketing of
such products as "earth friendly" in this context should be repug-
nant to environmentally conscious consumers.

The Bottom Line

෴ Seaweed extracts contain plant growth regulators, which, like traditional rooting products, can stimulate root growth in cuttings and transplants.

෴ Seaweed extracts have no reliable effect on plant production or resistance to disease and environmental stress, especially under field conditions.

෴ Variations in plant materials and environmental conditions are greater determinants of plant health than applications of seaweed extract.

෴ Kelp forests are the mainstay of coastal ecosystems whose stability is jeopardized when they are harvested.

෴ Because seaweed extracts represent luxury use of a natural resource and have little practical value, their use in gardens and landscapes is not recommended.

References

Abbey, T., and T. Rathier. 2005. "Effects of mycorrhizal fungi, biostimulants and water absorbing polymers on the growth and survival of four landscape plant species." *Journal of Environmental Horticulture* 23(2): 108–11.

Dixon, G. R., and U. F. Walsh. 2004. "Suppressing *Pythium ultimum* induced damping-off in cabbage seedlings by biostimulation with proprietary liquid seaweed extracts." *Acta Horticulturae* 635:103–6.

Gilman, E. F. 2004. "Effects of amendments, soil additives, and irrigation on tree survival and growth." *Journal of Arboriculture* 30(5): 301–10.

Jayaraj, J., A. Wan, M. Rahman, and Z. K. Punja. 2008. "Seaweed extract reduces foliar fungal diseases on carrot." *Crop Protection* 27(10): 1360–66.

Kelting, M., J. R. Harris, J. Fanelli, and B. Appleton. 1998. "Biostimulants and soil amendments affect two-year posttransplant growth of red maple and Washington hawthorn." *HortScience* 33(50): 819–22.

Malaguti, D., A. D. Rombola, M. Gerin, G. Simoni, M. Tagliavini, and B. Marangoni. 2002. "Effect of seaweed extracts-based leaf sprays on the mineral status, yield and fruit quality of apple." *Acta Horticulturae* 594:357–59.

Orquin, R., M. Abad, P. Noguera, R. Puchades, A. Maquieira, V. Noguera, and F. de la Iglesia. 2001. "Composting of Mediterranean seagrass and seaweed residues with yard waste for horticultural purposes." *Acta Horticulturae* 549:29–35.

Prokkola, S., P. Kivijarvi, and P. Parikka. 2003. "Effects of biological sprays, mulching materials, and irrigation methods on grey mould in organic strawberry production." *Acta Horticulturae* 626:169–75.

Sturz, A. V., D. H. Lynch, R. C. Martin, and A. M. Driscoll. 2006. "Influence of compost tea, powdered kelp, and Manzate 75 on bacterial-community composition, and antibiosis against *Phytophthora infestans* in the potato phylloplane." *Canadian Journal of Plant Pathology* 28(1): 52–62.

Zhang, X., E. H. Ervin, and R. E. Schmidt. 2003. "Plant growth regulators can enhance the recovery of Kentucky bluegrass sod from heat injury." *Crop Science* 43(3): 952–56.

Original article posted in November 2005.

THE MYTH OF
THE MAGIC BULLET

The Myth

"Success in the lab guarantees success in the field."

Managing landscapes sustainably requires, among other things, reducing the use of harmful chemicals in the form of fertilizers and pesticides. This has led to a surge in environmentally friendly products on the market that purportedly work as well or better than traditional pesticides. One of these products is harpin, a protein isolated from the bacterium (*Erwinia amylovora*) responsible for fire blight on fruit trees. This compound stimulates the biochemical pathways responsible for disease resistance in laboratory plant systems through a process called systemic acquired resistance (SAR). Since I have received several inquiries regarding the efficacy of this product on landscape plants, I obtained a

packet of the promotional materials for harpin marketed by Eden
Bioscience under the Messenger brand name.

The packet includes technical bulletins, a reprint of the *Science* journal article that first reported the existence of harpin,
experimental data developed by the company, testimonials from
gardeners, a CD entitled "The Science Behind Messenger Home
and Garden," an endorsement from the American Rose Society,
and a free sample of the product. The EPA fact sheet on harpin
confirms the low environmental risk and states that harpin protects "many crops, including vegetables, traditional agronomic
crops and ornamentals" against certain viral diseases, soil-borne
pathogens, and pests. Furthermore, the fact sheet continues,
harpin "reduces infestations of selected insects and enhances
plant growth, general vigor, and yield" of these same plants. The
EPA also bestowed their Presidential Green Chemistry Challenge
award on this product in 2000. It sounds like the "magic bullet"
that gardeners have been seeking.

The Reality

My first reaction upon reading the EPA fact sheet was that there
must be a solid body of scientific research to support the application of this material to the many plant species alluded to in the
EPA fact sheet. Upon contacting EPA regulators, I was surprised
to learn that efficacy data are not required for pesticide regulation: the concerns instead are focused on environmental and
human safety. While these are important criteria, it means that
the EPA depends on product manufacturers to supply objective
and accurate information regarding the effectiveness of their
products.

What Are the Specific Manufacturer Claims
for Harpin Efficacy on Garden and Landscape Plants?

Here are direct quotes from the sales literature provided with Messenger:

- "A 'vaccination' that naturally supercharges every plant in your garden."

- "Messenger treated plants are healthier, more vigorous, better able to resist stresses from adverse weather or pests, and are more productive."

- "Flowers, vegetables, shrubs, trees and even grass treated with Messenger turn up their natural growth and defense mechanisms empowering the plant to take up more nutrients, grow quicker and larger and have a stronger resistance to stress and disease."

There are many other absolute statements in the sales literature, which, when considered along with the *Science* reprint and EPA award, would lead any rational reader to assume that these statements had been scientifically validated. Since the informational packet contained no peer-reviewed studies documenting the success of harpin field applications, I turned to the scientific literature databases to answer my questions.

How Does Harpin Work?

This protein is thought to have its initial effect on the cell walls of the host plant. The most effective way to induce response is through tissue infiltration into the intercellular spaces (spaces between individual cells within a leaf or other tissue). Then, as the discoverers of harpin explain, "harpin elicits the [response] in many plants including tobacco, pepper, sunflower, tomato, cabbage, *Arabidopsis*, cucumber, geranium, watermelon and lettuce." This methodology works well with soft leaf tissues in a laboratory environment, but tissue infiltration is not a realistic application for whole plant work, especially in field situations.

Field application of harpin is subject to other practical problems as well. First, harpin cannot be mixed with chlorinated water, so users must have a source of deionized water. Second, users must be able to predict disease incidence or arrival of pest insects, since plants require five to seven days to become resistant after application of harpin. To overcome this problem, the manufacturers suggest applying the material every two to three weeks while the plants are growing—but at a suggested retail price of about twenty dollars per application, this can become a very expensive proposition. Third, some university researchers have suggested that climatic conditions will affect field success, where areas with longer growing seasons or higher levels of sunlight might exhibit greater success than cooler, shadier regions.

What Is the Current Science Behind Harpin?

≥ LABORATORY WORK. Less than a dozen crop species have been studied thus far for harpin activity, and nearly all of those studies have focused on cell culture or plant tissue responses. Experimental models such as these are useful for laboratory experimentation, but they have limited application to whole plant systems, especially those in uncontrolled environments. The results from such studies may not accurately predict what will happen in the field using the same species, and should not be used as indicators of effectiveness

on other species. Therefore, the numerous papers that have
focused on *Arabidopsis* and tobacco cell culture responses do
not provide reliable information in predicting harpin activity
in roses or any other landscape plant.

〜 GREENHOUSE AND FIELD WORK. The scientific literature with direct connections to landscape application of
harpin is limited to a handful of articles and includes primarily annual crop species (such as cotton, tomato, and
cucumber) and fruit trees (apple and citrus). The results here
were not positive; for example, harpin application did not
reduce tomato bacterial spot, control citrus canker, or
increase cotton crop production. I found no peer-reviewed
literature that reported consistent control of any pathogen
on any crop, or dependable evidence of improved growth
and/or yield. There are no laboratory or field studies on any
woody landscape species.

〜 TECHNICAL REPORTS FROM UNIVERSITY RESEARCH.
Though not as thoroughly vetted as published articles, technical reports from university research still can provide useful
and generally objective information. A number of fruits,
grains, and vegetables have been studied, including grapes,
strawberries, and tree fruits; peanuts and wheat; and cabbage, celery, corn, peppers, and spinach. In none of these
university studies was Messenger found to increase any quality or yield parameters, and in some cases actually reduced
yield. Likewise, Messenger provided little to no control of
disease. As with the published articles, none of these technical reports studied landscape plant species.

It is troubling that the EPA took none of the negative or inconclusive scientific data into account prior to releasing their fact sheet, which illustrates the conflict of interest inherent in allowing product manufacturers to submit efficacy information without external validation. As retired University of Kentucky Extension pathologist Dr. William Nesmith states, "The EPA assumes that the market place and lawyers will resolve issues related to poor efficacy. I urge growers to always ask for experimental data when considering disease control decisions." I would further suggest that you ask for experimental data from independent, scientific sources. If they are not available, take all "magic bullet" claims with a grain of salt.

The Bottom Line

~ Controlled laboratory experiments do not necessarily translate to greenhouse or field success.

~ Research on annual plant species does not necessarily apply to landscape trees and shrubs.

~ Harpin products have no demonstrated effectiveness on garden and landscape plants and their use is not recommended.

~ Don't succumb to advertising hype—get objective information before purchasing garden and landscape products.

References

Abbas, H. K., H. A. Bruns, and C. A. Abel. 2006. "Influence of Messenger on corn yield and mycotoxin contamination in Mississippi." Plant Management Network. "Plant Health Progress." http://www.plantmanagementnetwork.org/pub/php/research/2006/messenger/. Accessed September 10, 2008.

Becktell, M. C., M. L. Daughtrey, and W. E. Fry. 2005. "Epidemiology and management of petunia and tomato late blight in the greenhouse." *Plant Disease* 89(9): 1000–1008.

Boughton, A. J., K. Hoover, and G. W. Felton. 2006. "Impact of chemical elicitor applications on greenhouse tomato plants and population growth of the green peach aphid, *Myzus persicae*." *Entomologia Experimentalis et Applicata* 120(3): 175–88.

Bull, C. T., and S. T. Koike. 2005. "Evaluating the efficacy of commercial products for management of bacterial leaf spot on lettuce." Plant Management Network. "Plant Health Progress." http://www.plantmanagementnetwork.org/pub/php/research/2005/lettuce/. Accessed September 10, 2008.

Buschmann, H. Z., W. Fan, and J. Sauerborn. 2005. "Effect of resistance-inducing agents on sunflower (*Helianthus annuus* L.) and its infestation with the parasitic weed *Orobanche cumana* Wallr." *Zeitschrift für Pflanzenkrankheiten und Pflanzenschutz* 112(4): 386–97.

Jones, J. B., M. T. Momol, A. Obradovic, B. Balogh, and S. M. Olson. 2005. "Bacterial spot management on tomatoes." *Acta Horticulturae* 695:119–24.

Keinath, A. P., G. J. Holmes, K. L. Everts, D. S. Egel, and D. B. Langston Jr. 2007. "Evaluation of combinations of chlorothalonil with azoxystrobin, harpin, and disease forecasting for control of downy mildew and gummy stem blight on melon." *Crop Protection* 26(2): 83–88.

Obradovic, A., J. B. Jones, M. T. Momol, S. M. Olson, L. E. Jackson, B. Balogh, K. Guven, and F. B. Iriarte. 2005. "Integration of biological control agents and systemic acquired resistance inducers against bacterial spot on tomato." *Plant Disease* 89(7): 712–16.

Pradhanang, P. M., M. T. Momol, S. M. Olson, and J. B. Jones. 2005. "Management of bacterial wilt in tomato with essential oils and systemic acquired resistance inducers." In *Bacterial Wilt Disease and the Ralstonia solanacearum Species Complex*, edited by C. Allen, P. Prior, and A. C. Hayward, 133–38. St.Paul, MN: American Phytopathological Society.

Original article posted in April 2005.

THE MYTH OF
MILK AND ROSES

The Myth

*"Milk sprayed onto rose leaves will
prevent fungal and bacterial diseases."*

Recently, the Internet has been abuzz with the news that spraying milk on rose leaves can control foliar diseases. The Internet stories most often cite a Brazilian study published in 1999 focusing on powdery mildew control in zucchini. This new alternative to conventional fungicides has been augmented with anecdotal reports of successful powdery mildew control on a variety of plants, including roses. Moreover, the treatment is also touted as preventing leaf black spot, thus giving hope to rose aficionados everywhere of a safe, effective method of growing disease-free specimens.

The Reality

Milk has been part of the horticultural toolbox for many decades; for instance, it has been used with varying effectiveness as a spreader or sticker in pesticide applications. Perhaps the best-documented use of milk has been in reducing the transmission of leaf viruses, especially tobacco mosaic and other mosaic viruses. In fact, milk is routinely recommended as an organic hand sanitizer when handling virus-susceptible seedlings for transplant. Studies over the last half of the twentieth century report variable effectiveness of milk used for this purpose on a number of vegetable crops, as well as hibiscus (where it was effective) and orchids (where it was not).

How milk functions as an antiviral agent is not clear, but there are a few attractive hypotheses. First, milk may deactivate viruses chemically or isolate them physically; hence the success of milk as a sterilizing treatment. Second, milk may prevent aphid attack, and thus the transmission of aphid-borne viruses. Aphids may be deterred by the milk film on the leaf or attacked by aphid pathogens whose growth is enhanced by milk sprays; a 2003 study identified just such a fungal agent on treated pepper leaves.

Milk has made an appearance in recent literature as an antifungal agent, specifically in preventing powdery mildew in greenhouse- and field-grown vegetables. The results of these studies are variable and suggest that milk treatment under controlled (greenhouse) conditions is more successful than in the field. However, there have been no published scientific studies investigating roses or any other ornamental plant species.

In general, it appears that milk applied before fungal inoculation is more effective than milk applied after infection is present. Stems and lower leaf surfaces may be less protected, especially under high disease incidence. This last point is important when considering the value of anecdotal claims of the effectiveness of milk or any other pesticidal treatment. Unless plant material is actually exposed to the disease or pest of interest, it is impossible to attribute any subsequent lack of disease or pests to that treatment. Statements such as "Last year I had horrible black spot problems, but this year I used milk spray and my roses are disease-free" display faulty logic in the assumption of cause and effect where none may actually exist.

There are a few potential drawbacks to using milk as a foliar spray:

∾ Milk fat can produce unpleasant odors as it breaks down.

∾ The benign fungal organisms that colonize leaves and break down milk can be aesthetically unattractive.

∾ Dried skim milk has been reported to induce black rot, soft rot, and *Alternaria* leaf spot on treated cruciferous crops.

Is it worth trying milk as a treatment for viruses, powdery mildew, or any other disease? Absolutely! There is substantial evidence that milk treatments can be effective in the protection of some crops, and organic farmers especially might benefit from this method. But on which plant species will milk treatment prevent disease? What pathogens are actually inhibited by milk products, and which milk products are the most effective? Until these questions have been answered, it will be impossible to devise a reliable application protocol.

The Bottom Line

⁓ There is no evidence that milk sprays are effective in controlling black spot on roses or any other ornamental plant species.

⁓ Milk sprayed onto leaves may act as a nutrient source for benign microorganisms, decreasing the leaf area available for powdery mildew to infect.

⁓ Leaves coated with a milk spray may be less vulnerable to aphid attack, thereby reducing the transmission of aphid-borne viruses.

⁓ Milk sprays can encourage the growth of other microorganisms, whose presence may be aesthetically unappealing.

⁓ Milk sprays may be viable alternatives to conventional pesticides, especially for organic farmers.

References

Bettiol, W. 1999. "Effectiveness of cow's milk against zucchini squash powdery mildew (*Sphaerotheca fuliginea*) in greenhouse conditions." *Crop Protection* 18(8): 489–92.

Casulli, F., A. Santomauro, G. Tauro, M. A. Gatto, and F. Faretra. 2002. "Effectiveness of natural compounds in the suppression of the powdery mildew fungi *Sphaerotheca fusca* and *Uncinula necator*." *Bulletin-OILB/SROP* 25(10): 179–82.

Curtis, J. E., T. V. Price, and P. M. Ridland. 2003. "Initial development of a spray formulation which promotes germination and growth of the fungal entomopathogen *Verticillium lecanii* (Zimmerman) Viegas (Deuteromycotina: Hyphomycetes) on capsicum leaves (*Capsicum annuum* var. *grossum* Sendtn. cv. California Wonder) and infection of *Myzus persicae* Sulzer (Homoptera: Aphididae)." *Biocontrol Science and Technology* 13(1): 35–46.

Hu, J. S., and S. Ferreira. 1994. "Orchid viruses. Detection, transmission and management of cymbidium mosaic and odontoglossum ringspot viruses in *Dendrobium* in Hawaii." *American Orchid Society Bulletin* 63(8): 896–98.

Kamenova, I., and S. Adkins. 2004. "Transmission, in planta distribution, and management of *Hibiscus* latent Fort Pierce virus, a novel tobamovirus isolated from Florida *Hibiscus*." *Plant Disease* 88(6): 674–79.

Nagaraju, N., H. Jayaramaiah, B. N. Jagadeesh, and K. M. Channakrishnaiah. 2003. "Management of sunflower necrosis virus disease." *Plant Disease Research Ludhiana* 18(1): 85–87.

Original article posted in June 2006.

THE MYTH OF
WEED-KILLING GLUTEN

The Myth

"Corn meal gluten is an effective organic herbicide."

In terms of a holy grail, a safe and effective weed-and-feed product is what every gardener continually seeks. In the 1990s, such a product was reported and patented by researchers at Iowa State University. Corn gluten meal (CGM), the protein by-product of corn milling, is a high-nitrogen (10 percent), natural compound with documented success in reducing seed germination of many species. A pre-emergent herbicide, CGM inhibits root development during seed germination, at least partially by desiccating the soil and reducing water uptake.

Usage of CGM as a preplant herbicide and as a weed inhibitor in existing landscapes has exploded, especially within the organic gardening and farming communities. Corn gluten meal can be incorporated into the soil as a preplant treatment or broadcast over existing landscapes. Current recommendations for use include turf grass landscapes and commercial as well as residential small fruits and vegetable production. Though drawbacks of the product are occasionally mentioned (specifically its cost and lack of control over existing weeds), they are overshadowed by the promise of an all-natural magic bullet.

The Reality

The principal researcher and patent holder of CGM, Dr. Nick Christians, is cautious in his recommendation of CGM for weed control. He and his students and staff have published a number of papers in the scientific and popular literature. These researchers are careful to point out that CGM does not affect existing weeds, and that the nitrogen in CGM will benefit existing weeds as well as desirable plants. Therefore, inadequate weed removal prior to treatment can actually result in an increased weed problem.

CGM is not a selective product, nor is it effective on all weed types. Several species of weeds, flowers, and vegetables are inhibited by CGM, while others are not. Effectiveness in greenhouse trials generally increases with application rate (as does the cost).

While greenhouse trials outside of Iowa have demonstrated that CGM application can inhibit seed germination of a number of both weed and desirable species, field trials in these same locations often have not reached the same conclusions. University researchers in California and Oregon studying weed control of containerized plantings report that CGM had little effect on either broadleaf or grass weed species. Use of mulch was more effective, and subirrigation was the best weed control strategy of all. Similarly, both California and Oregon State researchers found no control of turf grass weeds by CGM, though the turf responded well to the addition of this high-nitrogen fertilizer.

Washington State University researchers found no differences in weed control on field-grown strawberries, though yield was slightly improved. The Iowa State group had similar disappointing results in their strawberry trials, with no significant differences in either weed control or strawberry yield, even after multiple treatments with CGM.

Why the disparate results between greenhouse and field trials, or between different climatic regions? Part of the reason may lie in the mechanism of control. Since the desiccation of germinating seeds is necessary for their demise, environmental conditions must first be perfect for seed germination and then for seedling death. Weed seeds require adequate levels of moisture, warmth, and light to germinate, and these factors vary among species. While it is relatively easy to control these conditions (and species composition) in the greenhouse, it is impossible to control them completely in a field situation. First, seeds germinate over the entire growing season, providing a continuous source of weeds. Second and perhaps most important, soil must not remain moist if CGM is to function as a desiccant. The Iowa State researchers found that "affected plants may recover and resume rooting" if the soil is moist enough to overcome the drying effects of CGM, and that a short drying period is critical between seedling germination and root establishment. In much of the coastal western United States, spring is generally the wettest season; hence it is not surprising that field-testing of CGM efficacy is not successful in these climates.

Finally, the cost of CGM is very high compared to other weed-control strategies. This is not a one-time control strategy. Iowa State University's research approach utilizes repeated applications throughout the season and from year to year. Recent prices on the Internet range from thirty dollars to forty dollars for a fifty-pound bag, not including shipping and handling. With a recommended application rate of twenty to forty pounds per 1,000 square feet, plus the need for repeated applications to improve effectiveness, costs can become prohibitive for all but the smallest landscapes.

Corn gluten meal does bind and release water, which may benefit a landscape in the drier parts of the year. It is also an excellent source of nitrogen, and a healthy lawn or landscape will be more resistant to weed invasion than an underfertilized site. But there are much cheaper ways to maintain soil moisture, provide slow-release nutrients, and control weeds than using a CGM product whose practicality thus far is questionable.

The Bottom Line

- Corn gluten meal (CGM) is a protein-based, natural product with potential pre-emergent herbicide activity.

- CGM has no negative effect on established weeds and can actually serve as a nitrogen fertilizer.

- CGM is not selective and can inhibit germination of desirable plant seeds as well as weeds.

- Though it may be effective in the Midwest United States, CGM is not as effective in other climate zones, such as those in the western United States.

❧ There are no scientific data from field trials in the western United States to support the use of CGM in weed control.

❧ Other environmentally friendly weed-control treatments (such as subirrigation, mulch, or soil solarization) are cheaper and often more effective than CGM.

❧ For these reasons, the use of CGM is not recommended, especially in regions with wet spring weather.

References

Gough, R. E., and R. Carlstrom. 1999. "Wheat gluten meal inhibits germination and growth of broadleaf and grassy weeds." *HortScience* 34(2): 269–70.

Hilgert, C. 2003. "Evaluation of natural and synthetic preemergence herbicides used in ornamental landscapes." Master's Thesis, Oregon State University.

Kuk, Y. I., N. R. Burgos, and R. E. Talbert. 2001. "Evaluation of rice by-products for weed control." *Weed Science* 49(1): 141–47.

Liu, D. L. Y., N. E. Christians, and J. T. Garbutt. 1994. "Herbicidal activity of hydrolyzed corn gluten meal on three grass species under controlled environments." *Journal of Plant Growth Regulators* 13(4): 221–26.

McDade, M. C., and N. E. Christians. 2000. "Corn gluten meal—a natural preemergence herbicide: Effect on vegetable seedling survival and weed cover." *American Journal of Alternative Agriculture* 15(4): 189–91.

Wilen, C. A., U. K. Schuch, and C. L. Elmore. 1999. "Mulches and subirrigation control weeds in container production." *Journal of Environmental Horticulture* 17(4): 174–80.

Wilen, C., and D. Shaw. 2000. "Evaluation and demonstration of corn gluten meal as an organic herbicide." Slosson Report 1999–2000. University of California at Davis.

Original article posted in June 2004.

INDEX

A

acidic soils. *See under* soils

acrylamide, 132-38. *See also* hydrogels

ACT (aerated compost tea), 190-94

acute stress, 25. *See also* environmental stress

adaptation, 8, 12, 187; to disturbance, 143; to dry conditions,
32, 66, 101; to seasonal
changes, 37; to soil conditions,
32, 62; of weeds, 68

aesthetics: of landscapes, 53, 101-2,
214-15; of mulch materials, 7,
125, 148, 167

agricultural methods, 10-11, 13,
110, 116, 197; alternative, 17-21,
126-29, 137-38, 212-15; conventional, 19; intercropping,
11-12, 14; misapplied to urban
landscapes, 30, 42, 120-21,
132, 143-46; polyculture, 11, 19;
traditional, 143. *See also* crop
production

airborne chemicals. *See* allelopathy

air pollution, 56

alkaline soils, 31-32. *See also* soils

allelopathy: growth suppression,
153; juglone, 154; thujaplicin,
155; thujone, 155; tropolone, 155

ABOUT THE AUTHOR

Linda Chalker-Scott is an Extension Urban Horticulturist and associate professor at Puyallup Research and Extension Center, Washington State University. She is the author of *The Informed Gardener* and the editor and co-author of *Sustainable Landscapes and Gardens*. She is the Washington State editor of *MasterGardener* magazine, author of the online column, "Horticultural Myths," and has a new blog, gardenprofessors.com.